Recasting Race
Women of Mixed Heritage in Further Education

Recasting Race
Women of Mixed Heritage in Further Education

Indra Angeli Dewan

Trentham Books

Stoke on Trent, UK and Sterling, USA

Trentham Books Limited
Westview House   22883 Quicksilver Drive
734 London Road   Sterling
Oakhill   VA 20166-2012
Stoke on Trent   USA
Staffordshire
England ST4 5NP

First published 2008

British Library Cataloguing-in-Publication Data
A catalogue record for this book is available from the British Library

ISBN: 978 1 85856 405 0

Cover picture: Leander Dewan

Designed and typeset by Trentham Print Design Ltd, Chester and printed in Great Britain by Cromwell Press Ltd, Trowbridge.

Contents

To Leander

Acknowledgements

I thank the women whose voices are represented in this book for being so open with their thoughts, opinions and feelings. Many other people have been directly and indirectly involved in its making. Sara Motta, Bob Cannon and Sharon Gewirtz gave feedback on various chapters, and Rosemary Harris proof read the final manuscript. Jocelyn Robson and Becky Francis supervised the PhD research on which this book is based. My discussions with these friends and colleagues, as well as many others I have not named, have much inspired my thinking over the last few years. My family, especially Heide and Gita, and my neighbours Bella and Tom, have given invaluable practical support. This book is dedicated to Leander – you have been patient, kind, and a *star* throughout.

Introduction
Unsettling norms, disentangling discourse

T his book is about mixed heritage women in further education in Britain. It arose out of a personal and political interest in the subject, and a concern about the palpable silence on this subject in academic and policy literature. By placing mixed heritage women centre stage, a space is opened up to critically interrogate some much vaunted theories and discourses around personhood and equity which are evident in contemporary sociological literature and education policy. The empirical data was taken from interviews with 40 mixed heritage women studying in Further Education colleges in ethnically diverse and mainly working-class areas of London, and from a selection of post-compulsory education policy documents published since 1997. Drawing on this data, one on mixed heritage identity, and the other on education, the book examines the relationship between theory, education policy and personal experience. The aim of the empirical investigation was to examine whether the women's identity constructions tallied with academic theories and popular discourses around mixed heritage identity and how their experiences and views on education corresponded with the UK government discourses on education.

The increasing number of mixed heritage people in Britain and changes in census policy to include mixed racial categories have coincided with a burgeoning literature on mixed heritage identity in the last decade (Wilson, 1987; Tizard and Phoenix, 2001[1993]; Ifekwunigwe, 1999, 2004; Alibhai-Brown, 2001; Parker and Song, 2001; Olumide, 2002; Ali, 2003; Gilbert, 2005). The literature has drawn largely on postmodern notions of identity to highlight the socially constructed, fluid and highly

1

complex nature of mixed heritage identities. This book contributes to existing research and knowledge around mixed heritage identity and further education but it also has a wider aim. Mixed heritage women and further education are the two lenses though which broader issues around race, identity, education, feminism and individualism are explored. *Recasting Race* seeks to expose and disentangle some of the theoretical, popular and policy assumptions around race essentialism, postmodern diversity and the dominant discourse of individualism. Race is the dominant theme of the book, both its tangible presence and its subtle absence.

The study has an antiracist feminist agenda. My premise is that racialised identities are the constructed product of historical, social and political processes, and unequal power relations render many mixed heritage women marginalised and discriminated against. In this sense, the personal arises out of historical and collective practices. I examine the ways in which the women's experiences may inform theory, and how theory can be used to further the feminist and antiracist emancipatory political project which seeks to advance equality and justice for women of mixed heritage and for all marginalised people.

Mixed heritage on the margins

Mixed heritage women are an important focus for research because they are marginalised in terms of race norms and male norms and are not accounted for in education research or policy. In terms of race norms, mixed heritage people are peripheral in relation to normative whiteness and other homogenous race categories, as they traverse two or more racial and cultural boundaries. Within popular discourse seemingly contradictory positions can be identified. On the one hand, despite the formal endorsement of mixed race identity through the 2001 'mixed' census category option, mixed heritage people are still often understood as either mono-heritage (Mahtani and Moreno, 2001; Alibhai-Brown, 2001) or as occupying an in between status. These understandings support the traditional view of mixed heritage people as black, marginal, out of place, and confused about their racial identity (Root, 1996; Ifekwunigwe, 1999). On the other hand, mixed heritage people are heralded as embodiments of a culturally diverse and race free society.

The recent report *Understanding the Educational Needs of Mixed Heritage Pupils* (DfES, 2004) supports the first position and shows that there is a tendency to view black Caribbean/white children as black or else to regard them as 'caught between two worlds' in which they are neither black nor white (p55). This publication, which focuses on the educational needs of mixed heritage children, reveals that some teachers had low expectations of mixed heritage pupils based on race stereotypical assumptions about barriers to achievement. These assumptions were that mixed heritage pupils had 'mixed up' and 'confused' identities (DfES, 2004, 50), and problematic family backgrounds – specifically absent black fathers and white single mothers unable to deal with issues relating to mixed heritage identity (p52). Because of 'identity problems' (DfES, 2004, 50) and peer pressure to adopt the norms of black youth sub-culture, mixed heritage boys especially were seen as more likely to adopt 'extreme' behaviour to prove their blackness (p55-56). This report indicates that further research on mixed heritage identity which specifically examines the interplay between race, class and gender in relation to education is needed.

The second position is underpinned by the view that mixed heritage people personify the postmodern condition: this popular discourse has developed as second and third generation children of immigrants grow up here, and notions of identity as pluralistic and fluid have become commonplace (Parekh, 2000). Mixed heritage people have often been proclaimed as epitomising the postmodern subject in that they can access and move between different cultures. As possessors of two cultures at least, they are celebrated as harbingers of a more egalitarian and progressive society, cultural bridge builders who have the potential to cure society of its racial ills. Mahtani (2002) has described this celebration of mixed race identity:

> It has also been assumed that the 'mixed race' individual has the solution for the world's racist problems in a vacant celebration of sanitised cultural hybridity, where the mixed race person is seen as a 'rainbow child' glimmering with hope for a colour-blind future. (p470-471)

Although this appears to be a harmless position, it has a pernicious side: mixed race people come to represent cultural harmony in society, the embodied evidence that problems relating to race relations are a thing of the past. In this process, culture is substituted for race: culture is understood as the inoffensive and superficial overlay to the individual who is quintessentially the same as and equal to everybody else. One consequence of an emphasis on difference defined as benign variation rather than conflict is that racial politics are ignored and the effects of power are rendered invisible. This results in 'harmonious, empty pluralism' (Mohanty, 2003, 191) in which mixed race people become symbols of a raceless future. It also constructs mixed heritage people as pedagogues, and as Camper (2004) has pointed out 'leaves the race work up to mixed people' (p181). Paradoxically, the idea of the munificent mixed heritage person draws on a discourse of race biological mixing, and in this instance, the mixing of two homogenously defined races. Sanchez (2004) has warned that investing 'utopian power in the genetic mixing of our era only serves to heighten a new form of race essentialism and once again frame the process of overcoming racial hierarchy as a fundamentally biological one' (p277). This new biologism is increasingly being used to answer questions about who we are, and there is a growing willingness to think about differences between people in biological terms (Skinner, 2004). Race essentialism and postmodern diversity therefore sit smoothly side by side in popular discourse: mixed heritage women are seen as representing the archetypal multicultural identity where this identity utilises and reinscribes essentialist categories.

Categories of race and gender are not embodied identities, but arise out of and are continually changing in relation to social processes. There is nothing essential about mixed heritage – it does not stem from two or more putatively undifferentiated race categories, nor does it embody harmonious cultural diversity. I have tried to avoid the imposition of normative categories in both the sample selection and the types of questions asked in the interviews. Because mixed heritage women defy normative race categorisation, and virtually no research has been done on mixed heritage women in relation to education, an important aspect of this investigation is to let the data speak for itself in order to create openings for new constructions and understandings of mixed heritage identity.

In terms of male norms (Walkerdine, 1990), a focus on women may have implications for a gendered account of mixed race people's ex-

4

periences. Whether and to what extent the women have internalised the post-feminist ideology, especially the idea that feminism is obsolete because women have achieved equality with men, is of particular interest to me (Whelelan, 1995). Post-feminism is a discourse which arose in the 1990s and marginalised feminism, constructing women as independent, successful and equal to men. It developed with the declaration of girl-power, which heralded an assertive femininity and paved the way for considerable new opportunities and freedoms for women (McRobbie, 2000). In education there certainly have been advances for women due to feminism and other developments in education and family systems (David, 2003). National results show that girls perform better than ever before in schools, even in subjects such as maths, science and technology (Francis, 2000), and that ethnic minority girls out-perform ethnic minority boys (Gillborn and Mirza, 2000).

The issue of mixed heritage women in education warrants urgent investigation because of the dearth of research and literature in this area. Some research exists on mixed heritage pupils in secondary education (DfES, 2004), and the government's consultation document *Aiming High: Raising the Achievement of Minority Ethnic Pupils* (DfES, 2003) contains measures to raise the achievement of ethnic minority pupils and recognises the under-performance of mixed heritage pupils. However, no research has been done on mixed heritage identity in relation to the further education sector. Few publications are dedicated to student social identity within this sector per se (except for Leathwood, 1998 and Colley *et al*, 2003). Given that the FE sector has been expanded due to widening participation initiatives, this gap in the literature is surprising although not unexpected because FE remains the poor relation of the education system and does not generate the same academic interest as HE.

The absence of mixed heritage identity is also patent in terms of education policy. This is also not surprising given the increasingly universalistic position on identity in education policy. Whilst the policies of the 1980s (DES, 1981; DES, 1985) took a multiculturalist stance, more recent policy has adopted an individualist universalist position on personhood (DfEE, 1998, 1999). The multicultural ethos is a liberal particularist position which assumes that people belong to particular cultural groups all deserving equal recognition, and that although people may be culturally different, they have the same opportunities as everyone else. The current liberal universalist position focuses on the rational individual functioning within a democratic egalitarian society. The universalist ideology has increasingly shifted to subsume the particularist ideology, where this is justified by the discourse of cultural assimilation. Within this universalistic framework, the idea that groups of people have distinctive sets of interests is seen as problematic and differentiated approaches to policy making are deemed unnecessary (DfEE, 1999).

Educationalists have been concerned with the existing universalist perspective and the discrepancies between the government's purported policy intentions and their actual outcomes. They have drawn attention to the initiatives aimed at promoting equality of opportunity and social inclusion which are couched within a benign new liberal language, and to the government's failure to address broader inequalities and issues relating to the widening gap between rich and poor (Lister, 2001). They have pointed out that failure and achievement is legitimated by the culture of meritocracy and responsibility to the self, and that the discourse of education as both a right and a duty puts the onus on the individual to take up the opportunities on offer or to be socially excluded (Tight 1998a, 1998b; Lister, 2001; Colley and Hodkinson, 2001; Mizen, 2003).

The dominant discourses of individualism, post-feminism and post-modernism would have us believe that we are rocketing towards an egalitarian, meritocratic and race free society in which everyone has the same chances and that structural inequalities based on race, class and gender do not exist. These assumptions are further complicated by the construction of mixed heritage people as the messengers of such a society, a responsibility imposed upon them because they straddle cultures, and must therefore be free from prejudice.

But how did the women position themselves *vis-á-vis* these discourses? Did they reflect or challenge academic and popular discourses, and how? Was race a dominant feature in their talk, or a marginal issue? Did they believe that they were equal to others, and equal to men? Did they feel they had reaped the benefits of widening participation initiatives in education? Were there any aspects of their lives where they felt discriminated against, excluded, or treated differently?

And what are the implications of these findings for feminist politics? Some feminist academics have argued that mixed race people do not want to define as black, that there is a fundamental desire for a mixed race category and that mixed race people are already producing their own cartographies of identity (Ifekwunigwe, 1999; Mahtani *et al*, 2001). Ultimately, the intensification of individualism and associated discourses such as post-feminism encroach on the possibility for solidarity and collective action. As McRobbie (2000) has pointed out, assertive femininity is far from being evidence of feminism: it simply reveals how far a popular version of feminism 'can be pulled in the direction of the political right, where the values of brutal individualism and the pursuit of wealth and success turn all personal and social relationships into an extension of the market economy' (p211). Did the women feel that issues around race and gender equality were relevant to them, or that there was anything left for mixed heritage women as a group to fight for? Was there any desire for a category or collectivity of mixed race? Was there a common experiential denominator amongst the women which was grounded in their experience of being mixed race? And whether or not the women believed that feminism was needed, could a feminist project even develop at all in this climate of individualism and at a time in which people feel that they do not have the power to change things and are increasingly alienated from politics?

The ideas that have been explored so far in relation to mixed heritage women and education can be understood within the framework of the sociological theories and discourses of essentialism, postmodernism and individualism. In the next section I explore these theories and clarify my own theoretical position on the subject of race.

Interrogating race: essentialism, postmodernism and individualism

In sociology, cultural studies and feminist studies, one of the key debates has focused on the relationship between essentialism and postmodernism, particularly in the field of gender. This debate is about whether biology (nature) or society (nurture) determines who we are. In basic terms, essentialist identities are distinct and static, whilst postmodern identities are multiple and fluid. The nature, or essentialist, side claims that social differences and inequalities have a biological basis and that males and females are naturally inclined to think and behave differently (Bordo, 1989). Essentialism is described by Burr (1995) as

> a way of understanding the world that sees things (including human beings) as having their own particular essence or nature, something which can be said to belong to them and which explains how they behave. (p19)

The nurture, or social constructionist/post-structuralist argument, asserts that gender differences are constructed by environmental factors (Butler, 1990, 1993). Whilst feminist debates have centred around the *impasse* between essentialism and constructionism in relation to gender, essentialism has for the most part been discredited in relation to race, and critiques of race difference have unambiguously focused on its socially constructed character. Postmodern and post-structuralist philosophy has been useful in providing a framework for understanding how identities are nuanced, flexible, subject to change, and positioned through discourse. These ways of thinking go beyond the rigid essentialism which is based on the idea that identities are pre-determined, and that people possess fixed racial traits which unite them with those of a particular race and differentiate them from all others (Anthias and Yuval-Davis, 1992; Hall, 1992; Brah, 1996).

The notion that race is not real is now somewhat hackneyed in academic fields, and few social scientists and educationalists would refute this claim. This idea has also served education policy makers well: it underscores the idea of the rational individual who is equal to all others and who is able to make unencumbered choices within a meritocratic society. Yet at the same time race is reified through dis-course, and race thinking remains trenchant (Gilroy, 2000). Although it has been widely acknowledged that there is as much genetic variation within races as between them (Gist and Dworkin, 1972), the association between race, biology and phenotype remains a popular and pervasive one (Small, 1994; Ifekwunigwe, 1999). Moreover, asymmetric relations of power continued to constitute hegemony, racial hierarchies and in-equalities along black/white lines (Mac an Ghaill, 1999). In recent years we have also seen a rise in genetic and genomic constructions of race, and the ways in which race is understood correspond with the ways in which the relationship between human beings and nature is being constructed under the influence of the DNA revolution (Gilroy, 2000; Skinner, 2004).

The dilemma is how to talk about something which is everywhere, and yet does not exist. The main difficulty with using the term race is that it is based on an assumption about its scientific validity. The consensus amongst many academics is that there should be no importance attached to *race* as a biological category but that the prevalence of *racialisation* should be acknowledged (Gilroy, 1993). Racialisation concerns the processes by which race is constructed historically and the ways in which these constructions underlie race exclusionary practices. The main argument for this position is that in disbanding race as a meaningful concept, we are left with an 'uncompromisingly romantic reassertion of liberal individualism which ignores socially constitutive effects on the person such as racism and racial ascription' (Parker and Song, 2001, 12), and no tools with which to combat social inequalities. If we remove race from the agenda, we cannot at the same time claim that race prejudice, social ascription, marginalisation and discrimination exist, and challenge such inequities in society.

Whilst I wholly reject essentialism as a theory, it is important to retain the concept of race in order to understand its significance in people's lives. Race is a product of discourse without inherent meaning in itself, and it is only through the meanings ascribed to it, and an understanding of how discourses around race are produced, that sense can be made out of the women's articulations around race.

The other key theory discussed in this book is individualism, or individualisation. Some social theorists have argued that traditional identities such as class, race, community, family and nation, are gradually being replaced by a process of individualisation which emphasises individual choice and a culture of the self (Beck and Beck-Gernsheim, 2001). Individualisation is symptomatic of a pluralised and fragmented society, in which modern identities are fluid and disjointed, and people refer to themselves in terms of different versions of themselves which operate in different contexts (Beck and Beck-Gernsheim, 2001, 23). Condemned to activity, the person seeks self-enlightenment and liberation, and is self-consciously concerned with securing a life of her or his own in the name of a new ethics which Beck and Beck-Gernsheim (2001) have called 'duty to oneself' (p38). This duty to oneself is symptomatic of the 'paradox of institutional individualism' (Beck and Beck-Gernsheim, 2001, 23) in which the interests of the individual and rationalised society are merged. Rose (1992) explains this phenomenon:

> Become whole, become what you want, become yourself: The individual is to become, as it were, an entrepreneur of itself, seeking to maximise its own powers, its own happiness, its own quality of life, through enhancing its autonomy and then instrumentalising its autonomous choices in the service of its lifestyle. (p150-151)

From the constructionist viewpoint of this book, essentialist, postmodernist and individualist theories and discourses do not manifest themselves in mutually exclusive ways: a complex picture of overlapping, contradictory and sometimes supporting discourses and theories emerges. This suggests that the seemingly oppositional discourses of individual responsibility and race biology may be mutually inclusive.

Discussing discourse

Discourse analysis is the methodological cornerstone of this book. It makes it possible to see how dominant discourses such as essentialism, postmodernism and individualism, which structure the way we think about things and appear to be a reflection of reality, are embedded within the women's praxis of language and policy discourses. Discourses are actively working practices which position people in particular ways and present particular relations as self-evident. Language and discourse do not neutrally reflect reality or tell truths about the world, but rather construct reality, presenting it as if it were true or natural. This construction is intimately linked to power (Foucault, 1979). We cannot stand outside discourse but, rather, we perpetuate discourses in that they speak through us. As Parker (1992) puts it: 'A strong form of the argument would be that discourses allow us to see things that are not 'really' there, and that once an object has been elaborated in discourse it is difficult not to refer to it as if it were real' (p5). Therefore, race is real because it is a discourse in society, and has real effects.

The role of discourse and how it constructs social phenomena, categories and ideas is analysed. A discourse analytical approach allows us to see how power and inequality operate: it enables us to identify many taken for granted assumptions, and reveal the causes and connections that are hidden. It permits us to look below the surface and see the ways in which mixed heritage women's subjectivities and experiences are discursively produced and located in the ways in which they understand their own social positions and racial identities.

Some feminists have pointed out that the difficulty with the discourse analytical approach is that although it shows how power operates, power is not seen to be held by some at the expense of others but is always relative to context. Therefore any universal accounts of oppression, including the patriarchy, cannot be recognised (McNay, 1992). Despite this limitation, I do not believe that discourses are simply relative to each other and there is no truth in discourse: people are located within asymmetrical power relations which are constructed through discourse and which have real effects.

A more significant problem with the discourse analytical approach is that it draws on the idea that personal experience, theory and policy are mutually informative. They are cyclical and reproductive rather than linear and productive. The difficulty is that this cyclical pattern is hard to break because many people are not aware of the ways in which discourses affect them. This is especially true in the present climate of individualism, in which the interests of the individual and society merge.

This book has an antiracist feminist agenda: many mixed heritage women are positioned by race and gender discourses, and are affected by the historical, social and political processes of marginalisation. However, given the dominance of the principles of (masculine) individualism and post-feminism, we might expect a sense of satisfaction with education and a lack of critical engagement with government discourses. Therefore, whilst feminist theory is useful for developing emancipatory concepts and strategies, does it have any practical relevance in women's lives today? If the women say they are content, and claim they do not need antiracist feminist practice, then do we simply accept this? If experience spoken through language is simply a product of theoretical, popular or policy discourse, and the women's talk merely reproduces the discourses of race essentialism, post-feminism and individual responsibility, how can new knowledge based on their experiences be created, and push theory and policy forward?

Dominant discourses and ideas about what is normative are deeply entrenched within our psyches and lifestyles. The current era of the de-politicised individual, the demise of collective forms of political action, and what Giroux (1988) calls 'normative pluralism' in which people occupy different but equally valid places in society, is not conducive to alternative modes of thinking and collective action. Even with an awareness of the harmful effects of discourse, we need to find ways to overcome rooted notions of what is normative and work in practical ways towards abolishing social and economic injustice. In the final part of this book critical pedagogy is explored as one possible way out of the limitations of discourse. Critical pedagogy enables us to disentangle dominant discourses, analyse how experience is constructed and legitimated, and create alternative oppositional discourses.

Structure of the book

Chapter One discusses the research process. Chapter Two gives an account of existing sociological studies and popular discourses around mixed heritage identity, and explores theories of feminism in relation to mixed heritage. These studies, discourses and theories provide a framework for the women's talk on identity which is explored in Chapters Three to Five. These three chapters examine the women's self-perceptions of identity, and issues around friendship and adapting; experiences of categorisation, difference and discrimination; and identity transformations.

Chapters Six to Eight focus on the theme of education. Wider UK government discourses, and discourses around personhood and equity identified in the selected policy documents are compared with what the women in the study said on education. This follows Ozga's (1990) view that it is crucial to 'bring together structural, macro-level analysis of education systems and education policies and micro-level investigation, especially that which takes account of people's perception and experiences' (p359).

Chapter Nine draws together key themes around identity and education. The interplay between postmodernist, essentialist and individualist discourses and the paradoxical ways in which the theme of race was talked about are discussed. Finally, I consider the implications of the research findings for a feminist political project which has mixed race women and their education in mind, and explore possible ways to develop education policy and practice that is more equitable.

1
Routes of the research

This chapter introduces the women and the research field, and discusses the methods used in collecting and analysing the data, and some of the issues and problems which arose during the research process. It also examines the discourse analytical approach in greater depth, and how it was used to gather and analyse the two sets of data.

The women

The sample consisted of 40 women who identified as mixed race, including five with whom the questions were piloted. All the women interviewed were approached in FE college environments in inner London in 2001 and 2002. The three main criteria for selection were that the respondent must be female, identify as mixed heritage, and either be a student or have been studying at an FE college in London in the last five years.

Over half the women interviewed were first generation black or ethnic minority/white. One woman had been adopted by two white parents. Five women were by standard definitions second generation mixed heritage, and five had dual ethnic minority parentage, such as Egyptian-Eritrean, or same-continent parentage, such as English/Turkish. Five women were classified as multiple heritage, meaning that they had more than two racial heritages and neither parent was white. Thus Anabel, who described herself as Guyanese/Indian-White was classified as multiple heritage. Such classifications have limitations and should not be taken too seriously. Jennifer, who described herself as Caribbean-Portuguese-Asian/English-Irish, could be classified as multiple heritage but was classified as first generation mixed heritage because she had one white parent. Many respondents were precise about their exact racial mix – traced back to parents, grandparents, and great grandparents. The way in which the women described their heritages is how they are presented in this book. Therefore Nalia is described as three quarters Black and a quarter Chinese, and Kim as African (Cuban-Jamaican) and English.

The women's ages ranged from 16 to 44, many had dependants, many were in part-time or full-time work and none had a disability. Around two-thirds had been brought up in one-parent households, usually with the mother. In two cases the mother was absent or marginal. The women were not specifically asked how they perceived their class backgrounds. Few referred to themselves as working-class, and none as middle-class. Given that most of them lived in working-class areas of London, and that traditionally many more working-class than middle-class people access further education, it is likely that most of the women were from working-class backgrounds. Skeggs (1997) found that whilst the working-class women in her study recognised their position within the class hierarchy, they simulated lower middle-class positions in their narratives about who they were. Olumide (2007) recently highlighted the importance of understanding mixed race experiences in relation to class:

> Whilst the well educated and more privileged members of the mixed race 'community' are free to explore, like their US cousins, their individual responses to being mixed race ... there are others who receive disproportionately negative experiences and appear, in consequence, to be particularly disadvantaged – more so than those in 'mono-racial' groups. (p29)

It seems likely that many of the women in this study saw themselves as neither 'better educated and affluent' nor as 'poorer and less educated' (Beck and Beck-Gernsheim, 2001, 38) but as somewhere in between.

This investigation is framed within a context in which increasing numbers of working-class people are becoming students largely due to government widening participation initiatives, and new discourses around race, youth and education which enable working-class people to define themselves as students. The discursive parameters of who can call themselves educated is therefore shifting. Nearly all the women in this study were the first in their families to access any form of post-compulsory education. Whilst a broader analysis of the ways in which the women were positioned by class discourses is outside the remit of this study, the environment within which the women in this study grew up, whether in mixed, or predominantly white or black working-class or middle-class environments, inevitably had an impact on the discourses available to them in

- their constructions of selfhood and education

- the degrees of marginalisation or privilege they experienced

- the educational resources and opportunities accessible to them.

It was surprising that only two respondents chose a pseudonym. This may have been an indication that they wanted their own voices to be heard, or it may simply have been a reflection of our Big Brother times in which privacy is less and less revered, and everything is everyone's business. Some of the women's quotes in this book may be seen as controversial. Ten women have been given pseudonyms to protect their identities.

On the term 'mixed race'

Like the term race, the term mixed race has been criticised because it presupposes a valid scientific foundation and suggests that mixed race identity arises out of two pure or original races; it also assumes that mixed race people automatically identify with two races which are differentiated from each other. Some academics have grappled with finding a more appropriate term to encapsulate the mixed race experience. In the States, for example, multiracialism (Root, 1996; Chiong, 1998; Winters and DeBose, 2003), and biracialism (Rockquemore and Brunsma, 2002) are popular terms to describe people of two or more racial heritages. Although one recent publication refers to mixed heritage pupils (DfES, 2004), and another uses the terms metise(se) and metissage in an attempt to incorporate generational, ethnic and cultural concerns (Ifekwunigwe, 1999), the term mixed race has never been seriously challenged in the UK.

Compared with these semantic difficulties in describing people of mixed heritage, the women in this study seemed well acquainted and unperturbed by the term mixed race. In response to the question: *How do you feel about the term mixed race?* only two women were ambivalent, but they still used the term. Ruby (Punjabi Indian/Irish) was concerned about its biological connotations, and suggested that 'mixed origin' might be a better term. Danielle (English/Jamaican) found mixed race an offensive label but used it because it was commonly understood:

> It's just something you have to do in order for people to know, basically to identify a person to know what they're talking about. It's a bit derogatory, because there are people who are not white or black, and they have to deal with it because they've been born in to it.

Several of the younger women in the study said they preferred the term half-caste to mixed race. This observation echoed research undertaken in 1990-1991 by Tizard and Phoenix (2001) who found that respondents preferred to use half-caste in informal contexts and to keep mixed race for formal use. Cassandra (Jamaican/Irish), who was 16 years old, was aware that mixed race was the more acceptable term, but chose to use half-caste:

> I don't use mixed race, I just use half-caste ... I've always used it, half-caste. Some people think it's racist, but most half-caste people I know don't think it's racist. Like, my dad says it's not a nice word to use.

Corinna said her friends used the term half-caste, but she herself criticised it:

> I'm happy about the term [mixed race]. Half-caste is like half-breed – mixed race to me is the nicest term. I never use the term half-caste, but now and then people use it and I find it hurtful.

Chantel (African/English) had a more casual attitude to terminology, using both half-caste and mixed race. The fact of mixed race was the important issue, not what it was named:

> If you look up race in the dictionary it tells you what it is. It's like what is a jumper? Just because you don't like the word jumper doesn't mean it's not a jumper. It's a jumper, it's mixed race.

Variations of the term mixed race such as mixed heritage, mixed parentage, dual heritage and biracial are as much dual constructions as the
term mixed race in that they are all premised on the idea that two races
and cultures are inherited. Olumide (2005) has convincingly argued
that the term 'mixed racialised'

> permits the defined to place the burden of race thinking at the feet of
> the race thinker. It conveys succinctly a social location within the
> 'seeing' society and, moreover, it suggests an awareness of social pro-
> cesses of racialisation that convey such distinctive social experiences.
> (p132)

The terms mixed heritage and mixed race are used in this book. Mixed
heritage is useful for referring to ideas which encompass notions of
race, culture, and heritage, and is often used when talking about
academic and popular concepts, theories and discourses. Mixed race is
how the women described and defined themselves and is widely understood and used in discourse, and this term is used when discussing the
women and their experiences. This is not to say that the use of the term
'race' validates the existence of distinct biological/racial categories
(Miles, 1989). Although the concepts of race and mixed race in this book
are referred to in seemingly unproblematic ways, there is nothing
natural or essential about race differences, and race, like all other categories and identities, are socially constructed through discourse.

For reasons of space and so as not to distract the reader from the main
issues being discussed, the specific heritages of every respondent are
not listed when several women are mentioned at the same time.
Despite the dangers of reductionism, the term 'black' is sometimes
used to refer to African, Caribbean, South American, South Asian,
South-East Asian or Arab heritage. Black has been used in academic
literature to describe people with one or both parents who descend
from Africa, the Caribbean, and in many cases Asia. It is often used as a
political category, and was a term created as a way of alluding to the
common experiences of racism and marginalisation amongst ethnic
minority people in Britain (Hall, 1992, 252). Although racial discrimination was an experience shared by most of the women in this study, I
am aware that the term black is inadequate as a description for all
people who have a heritage which is not white. This is especially so in a
study concerned with self-definition and not standard categories.

There is an important point to be made about the second generation and multiple heritage people who self-defined as mixed race but did not fit the standard definitions of first generation, black or ethnic minority/white, or dual ethnic minority mixed heritage. These self-definitions fly in the face of understandings of mixed heritage as a mixture of two or more pure races, and really expose the myth of race for what it is: pure fabrication. Nobody is pure anything, and we are all in some sense mixed.

In general, the second generation and multiple heritage women were darker than the first generation mixed heritage women who were interviewed. Rosa, who had three white grandparents, was an exception, and issues relating to her identity are discussed in Chapter Five. Perhaps these women defined themselves as mixed race and not as black out of recognition of their difference from so-called blackness. Certainly, they saw a connection between how they looked and their experiences of mis-categorisation and discrimination. Defining as mixed race may also have reflected the tendency in popular discourse to explain identity in multiple terms and to celebrate mixed heritage. As Jones (2004) has asked, with a dose of healthy scepticism: 'If it weren't such a fashionable and marketable identity these days, would so many folk be riding the bandwagon?' (p212). This is a question which may most aptly be applied to Paula, who some may argue was not mixed heritage because both her parents were from two 'white' European countries – Greece and Rumania. Paula was included in this study because she identified as mixed heritage, where a sense of difference on the basis of colour and religion were key factors, and because like most of the women she experienced discrimination. This case reveals the complexity around defining who is mixed heritage, and as third and fourth generation mixed heritage people grow up here, this issue will become ever more complex. The bottom line is that mixed heritage people who self-define as such, and who are assumed to be affected by the social and political consequences of racialisation or discrimination, may be understood as mixed heritage.

Negotiating fuzzy boundaries

Whereas physical access to the FE colleges was relatively unproblematic, social access to the students proved more difficult. Formal access strategies, such as trying to gain the co-operation of lecturers via contacts in the colleges, did not work. Email was the main form of communication. In retrospect, the lack of response was predictable given that college staff were probably inundated with emails on an hourly basis. I began approaching lecturers directly who, not surprisingly, had never heard of me or my proposed fieldwork. My aim here was to gain their permission to introduce my project to students in their lessons. Here too, I was unsuccessful in securing potential respondents. I ultimately gained access to my sample by talking to students directly in various college locations such as foyers and corridors, IT labs, libraries, canteens, and hairdressing and beauty salons.

This approach overcame the problems I had encountered earlier. Lecturers often did not know whether they had mixed race women in their classes. Talking directly to students meant that any queries they had could be dealt with directly, and it gave them a sense of privacy. In one instance I entered a classroom in which two mixed heritage women had been identified by their lecturer. However, when the lecturer asked whether there were any mixed race women in the class, neither of them had volunteered, even though they smiled and all their classmates looked at them. This illustrates the significance of context: the two women might have volunteered if approached directly in a less formal and public setting.

An important aspect of the investigation was to go beyond normative categories of personhood and question the stability of group identities generally. Although mixed race was used as a distinct category in approaching the sample, I wanted the women to ascribe themselves to make it possible to identify the differences between social ascription and subjective consciousness. My approach differed from Tizard and Phoenix (2001[1993]) who used normative categories of ethnicity as standards against which to measure self-definitions of identity in their study of mixed race children in a secondary school in the early 1990s. They maintained that the more diverse or unorthodox the findings, the greater the need for a normative framework to contain and analyse the data (Tizard and Phoenix, 2001). Whilst pre-set categories are useful for comparative analysis and may reveal how dominant discourses and categories are reflected in what people say and where certain tendencies lie, they restrict new understandings of mixed race identity which are not rooted in normative black, or black/white definitions of mixed race. The approach taken in this study resulted in a sample which was broad ranging in terms of racial identities.

Mixed race people are not easily identifiable, and in 2001/02 were a group for whom there was no statistical aggregate. The research involved purposive sampling even though women were rarely approached in the absolute knowledge that they were mixed heritage, and until they were approached it wasn't clear that their self-definition as mixed heritage made them relevant to the survey. Although most of those approached were gathered in mixed ethnic groups, many women were approached individually on the assumption that they were mixed heritage. This raised issues around self-selection and its impact on the voices represented.

One problem was that this hunch-based type of selection crucially challenged the principle of self-selection on which the research was based. Although there was no guarantee that approaching every woman encountered in the colleges would have yielded more representative results, my sample may have been different. The second difficulty was that I resorted to assumptions which challenged my own principles about categorising people according to appearance. Whilst personal perceptions about phenotype, skin colour and hair may give a correct reading of a person's self-defined racial heritage, it does not necessarily do so, and this was problematic from the social constructionist position of this book. However, it was important to be pragmatic, and to bear the overall purpose of the research in mind in negotiating the ethical difficulties around the identification of mixed race women. Ultimately, if the women had not liked being asked whether they were mixed race, the project would have been abandoned. But many appeared to be glad and even relieved to talk about their experiences of being mixed race, and there were no negative reactions from any of the women I approached, even those who did not identify as mixed race. From my own experience of being mixed race and growing up feeling that I had to keep both my heritages a secret to avoid ridicule, this did not surprise me. As the interview findings show, many of the women wanted to be recognised as mixed race – possibly because they had had a lifetime of being misrepresented, wrongly categorised, and discriminated against.

In selecting potential respondents I approached women who looked African/Caribbean and white, and brown people who might be Asian and white, or whose racial heritage was uncertain. Women were approached who had two parents from places including the Caribbean, Pakistan, Turkey, Brazil, Iran and Algeria. One college had a large number of Asian Muslim students and there were many women who may have been Asian/European, but there were no mixed heritage respondents amongst the women I approached. This may be explained by the relatively low percentage of South Asian/European partnerships compared with black African/white and black-Caribbean/white partnerships (Tizard and Phoenix, 2001).

The fuzzy boundaries of mixed race were encountered time and time again. There were women who did not fit the traditional definition of mixed race but who had two European, two African, or two Asian parents (for example, Turkish-English, Egyptian-Eritrean and Burmese-Mauritian) and self-identified as mixed race. It is also probable that some women who were mixed heritage by standard definitions did not identify themselves as such. Also, some second and third generation mixed race women identified themselves as mixed race, whereas most did not. It was initially tempting to discourage women who did not fit into clearly defined categories of mixed race from being interviewed. However, their self-identification as mixed race was a stark reminder that self-selection was an important criterion in terms of gaining access to data on self-ascription, as opposed to data which reflected normative categories. The ways in which the women self-defined as mixed race showed that definitions and discourses around mixed race are changing. Further research is required to shed light on these shifts in discourse.

The college setting: equality or difference?

In attempting to access the sample, I had many informal conversations with college staff which showed that race was a sensitive issue (Skeggs, 1994) and that the college space and those within it were largely seen as ethnically and racially neutral. This was perhaps a reflection of Britain's politically correct discourse around race. Using the terms mixed heritage and mixed race could make people who are unfamiliar with racial terms and concepts feel concerned about 'putting their foot in it' by appearing too race conscious and therefore politically *in*correct. Saying the 'wrong' thing, after all, could carry high costs. Other than the standard equal opportunities policies, there were no guidelines on how staff should manage the issues of race, ethnicity and culture. Prior to June 2005 few FE colleges had developed race equality policies (DES, 2003). Maybe because of the silence on race, some lecturers gave the impression that they wanted to talk about issues relating to race, but were not sure how to do it.

When lecturers were asked whether they had mixed heritage women in their classrooms they were being confronted with something they were not normally expected to think about within an institutional setting. Many white lecturers did not seem to know whether they had mixed heritage women in their lessons. This manifested itself in two different ways: some lecturers were cautious and non-committal on the subject of mixed race, whilst others zealously declared that they had many mixed race people in their lessons. Here is a typical account of what a white lecturer would say when asked whether s/he taught any mixed heritage women. Initially, the lecturer would say '*yes, I've got a lot of mixed race students in my class.*' Then, after a few seconds of perhaps trying to mentally picture these women, s/he would say, '*well actually, there are only a few ...*' A pause of another few seconds, and s/he would apologetically acknowledge '*well, perhaps there are only one or two ...*' And finally I would be told, '*actually, come to think of it, there aren't any.*' I soon learnt not to raise my expectations, and rather cynically began to predict the outcome of any conversation with a lecturer which began '*Yes, I've got a lot of mixed race women in my class ...*' This observation suggests that some lecturers had never given mixed heritage identity much thought. The lecturers responses perhaps reflect the current popular discourse which equates a diverse and multicultural society with a society that is well-populated with mixed heritage people, without necessarily having an understanding of mixed heritage.

The following more guarded comments were also typical: '*I really don't know what they are, it's not the kind of thing we ask*'; '*it's not the sort of thing we normally know*'; and, '*we treat everyone the same, race doesn't really come into it.*' Some white lecturers asked me '*how to put it*' when introducing my topic to their students. In contrast to white lecturers, the small number of black and mixed heritage lecturers seemed less anxious about talking about race issues. One mixed heritage lecturer simply strode into her classroom and asked the students straight up: '*Is there anybody here who is mixed race, from mixed parentage? No? Okay then. Thanks.*'

Conversations with white staff members revealed an unofficial discourse of personhood which looked beyond colour and possibly culture, and was concerned with the person *per se*. It was purportedly non-judgmental, and did not make assumptions or categorise. Although many of the lecturers claimed that they saw their students as equal, there was an abstract awareness of racial and cultural difference, but little understanding of what that meant. It is interesting that the dilemma which exists at ground level within colleges, which is how universal equality may co-exist with difference, is the same dilemma which preoccupies many sociologists, educationalists and political philosophers.

Approaches to the research

An interpretive and qualitative approach to collecting data was taken: this took the form of personal accounts of mixed race women's perceptions of identity and experiences of education. Discourses on identity and education in interview and policy texts were analysed, drawing largely on post-structuralist and feminist approaches to educational research. The theories and discourses of personhood identified in academic literature and policy documents were compared with the discourses articulated by the women on their constructions of self, their experiences of education in FE colleges, and their opinions of education policy discourses.

The development of the interpretive approach draws on several criticisms of positivism. Positivists claim that the social world, like the natural world, works in measurable ways and is therefore an objectively knowable place: they use mainly quantitative principles and methods to try to establish patterns and regularities in human behaviour. The interpretive model concentrates on discovering how meaning is made and how social practices are constituted within historical and cultural contexts. This model is concerned with multiple realities which are in constant flux, as opposed to the study of parts making up a finite whole. This study follows the interpretative approach in which accounts of the social world are representations, not reproductions (Hammersley, 1993).

An important way in which the positivist and interpretivist approaches differ concerns the relationship between the observer and the observed (Usher, 1996). In positivism the researcher and the researched are seen as separate entities: the researcher stands outside the research process and is understood to be a passive entity capable of rational objective thought. Within the interpretivist paradigm, the researcher is located directly within the research process and interpretive framework (Gadamer, 1975). Interpretivists have argued that our understandings of the world are subjectively constructed. Human beings are not passive agents, but are actively involved in defining and interpreting each other's actions (Blumer, 1986) so that the interactions of the people involved has an impact on the kind of data elicited. Because qualitative analysis relies on interpretation rather than statistics, the value and quality of the analysis hinges to a large extent on the experience and sensitivity of the researcher (Lincoln and Guba, 1985).

Researchers have pointed out that power relations and ideological suppositions inherent in the research process can hinder impartial research relations (Ball, 1993; Hornsby-Smith, 1993). Some feminist researchers grappling with this problem have sought to destabilise power relations and have striven for a more reciprocal relationship with the researched (Stacey, 1988). With this approach however, power relations are perceived not to exist, and some critics have argued that it diminishes the ability of the researcher to interpret critically and leads to bias in the interview (Schwandt, 1998). Interview bias is to some extent inevitable in qualitative research. Some feminist researchers view interview bias as a resource rather than a problem. This has led to debates around whether background knowledge is necessary for competent understanding of research subjects, such as whether only women can competently research women (Olesen, 1998), and how ethnic differences can impact upon researcher/researched relationships (Parker and Song, 1995).

In this research, implicit background knowledge was significant: gender was an immediate marker of commonality with respondents, as was colour. Often perceived similarities based on common experiences such as being mixed race, experiencing discrimination, being a student, a parent, or a single parent helped to generate rapport and create a comfortable interview situation, which influenced the type and quality of data gathered. Following Klatch (1987), I tried to find 'common threads' and negotiate the 'delicate balancing act between building trust and gaining acceptance while not misrepresenting my own position' (p77-82). However, assuming connections with people on the basis of shared background knowledge is a form of essentialism. It is an example of how essentialist discourses may work through us: how we are positioned by essentialist discourse and how this influences how we position others.

The format of semi-structured interviews appeared most suitable. Although unstructured interviews with open-ended responses can provide valuable insights into personal experiences and opinions, responses could not have been compared, coded and categorised in the same way as with more structured methods. Semi-structured interviews composed of set questions and open-ended responses allowed me to question respondents on precise meanings around self-definitions of identity with the benefit of retaining a structure to the interview questions. It generated data which enabled me to identify key discourses and themes in the interview and policy texts, and do some numerical counting.

At the time of devising the interview questions and conducting the interviews in 2001/02 there was little published literature on mixed race identity. The interview questions on identity arose from the existing literature, general theories and public discourses around race, culture and ethnicity, and my own experiences. Wider UK discourses around education, and the discourses around personhood and equity which were identified in the policy documents provided a framework for the interview questions on education. The policy discourses were found in a selection of three post-compulsory education policy documents published between 1997 and 1999: *Learning for the Twenty-first Century* (Fryer, 1997), *The Learning Age* (DfEE, 1998) and *Learning to Succeed* (DfEE, 1999). Several further education papers have been published since then. The policy *Success for All: Reforming Further Education and Training* (DfES, 2002) is similar in tone to *Learning to Succeed*, whilst *Further Education: Raising Skills, Improving Life Chances* (DfES, 2006) focuses on reform programmes for raising skills and the quality of teaching and learning within the FE system. Whilst the earlier document refers to the neo-liberal agenda and the inextricable link between 'social justice and economic success' (DfES, 2002, 2) which is also evident in the policy documents scrutinised in this book, the latter document focuses on skills development, with no mention of social inclusion.

The interviews consisted of some introductory questions, ten questions on identity and ten questions on education. The interviews were between 30 and 90 minutes long and all of them were recorded on tapes and subsequently transcribed. They took place in canteens, libraries, computer rooms, hair salons or in empty classrooms. The women were told they could retract any part of the interview if they wanted to.

Analysing the data

An explanation of how discourse analysis was applied to the interview and education policy texts follows. Post-structuralists such as Derrida and Foucault were forerunners of discourse analysis and believed that language constructs rather than reflects reality. Derrida (1976) proposed a radical 'de-centring of the subject' in which both the subject and text were understood as linguistic products, that 'all the world is text' which is discursively produced. It was not the 'knowing' subject who should be at the centre of the study of human sciences, Derrida argued, but the discursive practices which construct this subject. As such, no authentic, privileged or universal meaning can be reached.

The data from the interviews was summarised, and major discourses and themes identified (Silverman, 1993). In this study the relevant text is any meaning which is symbolically significant for the reader (Parker *et al*, 1999). In general, the analysis involved comparing existing academic, popular and policy discourses with the interview data to reveal where wider discourses were being reproduced in the women's talk. It was also important to look at how the women critically engaged with, and gave alternative meaning to dominant discourses, and how people pushed at the limits of what was socially constructed and tried to make something different or create counter-discourses (Nightingale and Cromby, 1999). However, the space the individual has in which to act outside the normative remit of discourse is severely restricted (Ball, 2000).

Some comparative analysis was made between first generation black/ white women and all other respondents, between first generation and second generation and multiple heritage respondents, and between intra-continental respondents and all other respondents. However, the differences between these groups did not merit an analysis on the basis of distinct categories.

The selected policy texts were analysed using content and discourse analysis (Scott, 1990; Burman and Parker, 1993). They were briefly con-textualised and examined for their broad intentions and rationale, and content analysis was used to scan the policy documents systematically for their references to personhood and equality. This involved some numerical counting and an analysis of how notions of personhood and equality were conceptualised and categorised. Content analysis is useful for identifying how policy concepts of personhood have changed over a short period of time; numerical counting can show proportions and give a measure of the orientation of a policy argument or intention.

Discourses which formed part of the dominant ideology around educa-tion were identified in the policy texts, and these were compared with the women's praxis of language. Francis (1999a) provides an example of a similar approach in which she used semi-structured interviews and participant observation in educational research to show how students' constructions of education and the discourses identified in education policy may be linked.

Foucault (1972) claimed that discourses are practices which 'systema-tically form the objects of which they speak ... they do not identify ob-jects, they constitute them and in the practice of doing so conceal their own invention' (p49). Discourse signifies an array of statements which represent the emergence of particular cultural and political practices, perceptions, and power relationships; discourse constitutes the social relationships of individuals and their actions as social agents in so far as these are relationships in which positions of knowledge, authority, and subjectivity are formed (Feuchtwang, 1990).

Discourse analysis is useful for showing how policy discourses are pro-duced and perpetuated by dominant discourses which structure the way we think about things and appear to be a reflection of reality. Re-flecting on the work of Foucault, Ball (2000) has argued that all policies are ideologically abstract: policy is never a complete thing, but a process which is always changing, involving the cyclical relationship between ourselves, policy and the state:

> We are the subjectivities, the voices, the knowledge, the power relations that a discourse constructs and allows ... In these terms we are spoken by policies, we take up the positions constructed for us within policies ... There is little opportunity for obvious adversial responses to this process of subjugation. And we have to note the de-centring of the state in this, discourse is non-reductionist. The state is here the product of discourse, a point in the diagram of power. (Ball, 2000, 1836)

The meaning of policy changes as intentions are re-worked in accordance with the changing interests of the state. For example, in contemporary Britain we need to be aware of and analyse the dominant discourses of neo-liberalism and management theory (Ball, 2000, 1837). Ozga (2000) has claimed that it is just as important to critique policy as to analyse it, and that policy texts are resources for analysis in terms of the messages they attempt to convey, whose interests they serve, their relationship to global, national and local imperatives, and what they are assumed to be able to do. Research for policy is about discourse and structure: 'policy as discourse understands policy as part of the dominant system of social relations ... [it] frames what can be said or thought' (Ozga, 2000, 94); it assumes the inalienability of globalisation within the policy agenda, and that increased economic competitiveness through increased education and training is the solution to the problem of social exclusion. Research on policy is about text and agency. It is 'the element of policy that can be worked on, interpreted and contextualised' (Ozga, 2000, 94) and it enables us to be critical of the policy agenda (p97). Text and discourse, agency and structure, therefore operate in a relational sense in policy.

In analysing the policies some of Ozga's (2000) questions from her analysis of the policy document *Excellence in Schools* may be helpful. The aim in this investigation is to identify discourses on personhood and equity in education.

■ What is the story being presented? (How is it different to what went before?) What is the logic/discursive construction of the argument in the text? What assumptions are made, what is the tone of the policy?

- What ideas and categories are presented regarding social exclusion/inclusion? What is absent, excluded, silent? How is my own thinking affected by knowledge that lies outside the text, i.e. the tendency to produce or reproduce disaffected groups and individuals?

- How does the text construct its subjects? How are learners constructed? Who is excluded by these constructions? What do these texts imply about the relationship between their subjects and the world society/globalisation?

The policy analysis identifies key themes relating to the 'stories' being presented, the tone of the policies, how people and categories are represented with regard to social exclusion/inclusion, and how the texts construct their subjects (see Ozga, 2000). The policy discourses are compared with the discourses identified in the interview data on education. But first the notion of mixed heritage must be examined.

2

Mixed heritage in academic and popular discourse

his chapter provides an overview of mixed heritage in literature
and discourse. It discusses the subject of mixed heritage in
academic literature and the ways in which understandings
around mixed heritage have shifted over the last few decades. It also
looks at how mixed heritage is portrayed in popular and media discourse in Britain today. Much recent literature on mixed heritage has
been written by feminists: the last part of the chapter engages with
some of the issues pertinent to mixed heritage in this context.

Mixed race people in Britain today

Until the 1990s the British government had only been concerned with
counting and categorising the main racialised and ethnic groups in
Britain. Mixed race was not an official identity and the categories available for mixed race people to choose on ethnic monitoring forms were
either mono-racial or 'other'. The introduction of mixed race as an official category in the 2001 census, the rapid rise in interracial partnerships and the ever increasing numbers of mixed race people in Britain
have challenged public perceptions which view mixed race people as
mono-racial.

Britain has not experienced a multiracial movement in the same way as
the US in recent years. This is perhaps because there has never been a
policy of hypodescent, otherwise known as the 'one-drop rule' which
was applied in the US at the turn of the twentieth century in which a

person with 'one drop' of black blood was regarded as black (Root, 1996; Alibhai-Brown, 2001), nor a significant black consciousness movement. New forms of identification spawned a mixed race political movement in Britain in so far as it provided the impetus for the government to take action on the mixed race issue. In the run-up to the 2001 census, focus groups and cognitive tests showed that mixed race people were in favour of a mixed race census category. This, with support from government departments and the Commission for Racial Equality, led to the introduction of the mixed race category in the 2001 census in Britain and the formal recognition of mixed race as an ethnic group.

As the number of mixed race people grows, there has been an increase in mixed race forums to give information or advice, or provide a space for people to share experiences and participate in common struggles for racial and social justice (Intermix and People in Harmony, UK). The 2001 census included mixed race options for the first time: these were White and Black Caribbean, White and Black African, White and Asian or any other mixed background.

Statistics published by the Office for National Statistics in 2001 indicated that the mixed heritage population had increased by more than 75 per cent since 1991 to 415,000. A new estimate following the 2001 census put the figure at 674,000. Consequently the Commission for Racial Equality, in its submission to the Office for National Statistics, recommended that ethnic monitoring should be based on self-definition. The recognition of mixed race as an official identity also brought the needs of mixed race children to the forefront of discussion, especially about their over-representation in care and the possible failings of social services.

The significance of age amongst the mixed race population cannot be underestimated. It has been asserted that the mixed race population is growing so fast in the UK that there are more mixed race people than people from any other ethnic background apart from white under the age of 16 (Owen, 2004). One recent estimate claims that 50 per cent of mixed race people in Britain are under the age of 15 and less than 3 per cent are over 65 (Aspinall, 2004). Other data show that of the total population of children under 4 in Britain, 25 per cent are black mixed and 20 per cent are other mixed (Schuman cited in Owen, 2001). Owen has pointed out that figures on the mixed race population could be skewed because some single white mothers in particular might emphasise their child's mixed or minority heritage, whereas the child at 18 might not identify as mixed race. The opposite could equally be true: a white parent might deny their child's mixed or minority heritage, which the child at 18 might assert.

In a public seminar Lewis (2004) made the point that the percentage of mixed race people in London is far higher, around 3 per cent in Greater London and around 4 per cent in inner London, than the national average of 1 per cent, and that 20 per cent of all the city's children under the age of 15 were mixed race.

Some younger women in the study talked about the prevalence of mixed race in London today. Kerry (English/Bajan, 21) explained that there were not many mixed race people when she was at school a few years ago, but that *five years down the line, most of my brother's friends [aged 13] are mixed race'*, and that most children in primary schools today *'have some kind of mix.'* For Kerry, this was an indication of changing attitudes towards mixed race relationships and people in the last five years. Charmaine (Jamaican/White, 16) talked about the change in attitude towards mixed race identity since she was a child:

> When I was young you was either black or white, they didn't really recognise mixed race as an individual colour in itself ... if you're in between then they don't, people didn't, recognise you at all, but I think now it is being recognised, now you can just say you're mixed race.

In terms of education and employment, recent data from the Women and Equality Unit (2004) showed that whilst people from almost all ethnic minority groups had low levels of qualifications, mixed heritage women had average levels. However, mixed heritage women were less likely to be in work than mixed heritage men, and had the highest rate of unemployment compared with all other ethnic minority groups. A recent Labour Force Survey showed that a relatively high percentage of mixed race people aged 16 to 24 had no qualifications, and a comparatively high rate of unemployment, similar to that of Pakistani, Black Caribbean and Black African people. It also showed that mixed race people were in lower status occupations compared with white British people.

Existing studies on mixed race identity

Few early studies exist of mixed race people. Until the 1990s their experiences were subsumed within those of black or ethnic minority people. No studies on mixed identity were published until the 1960s: these studies focused on how people of mixed heritage developed black identities. Research on black identity concentrated mainly on the experiences of marginality felt by black people. Research on racial attitudes and marginality from the 1930s through to the 1980s centred on doll studies. Early studies by Clark and Clark (1939, 1947) concluded that because the majority of black children preferred white dolls, they misidentified as white; these children had internalised society's rejection of them as black and had therefore rejected their own blackness.

The work of Robert Park has been influential in understanding the identities of marginalised groups in society. Park (1964) argued against the idea that people of different races had different personalities, yet he viewed mixed race people as pathologically unstable because of their marginalised and ambiguous position in society. He argued that this made them 'more enterprising than the Negroes, more restless, aggressive, and ambitious. The mulatto and the mixed blood are often sensitive and self-conscious to an extraordinary degree' (Park, 1964, 387).

Stonequist (1937) also believed that mixed race people experienced a marginal condition, which had three stages. First, mixed race children identify with and attempt to integrate into the dominant white culture but soon understand that they are not accepted by white society. Second, they identify with the minority group, whilst still desiring to belong to the dominant group. This results in ambivalence: the white group is alternately idealised and disparaged, and the black group is seen as both a safe haven from their oppression and a prison (see Katz, 1996, 22). Third, the person of mixed heritage assimilates into either the dominant group or the subordinate group, or finds a place between the two groups.

Poston (cited in Banks, 2002), in a study published in 1990, found that mixed race people went through a five-stage process in their development of an ethnic identity: initially there was no awareness of being mixed race; then the choice about which group to identify with was forced upon them and feelings of confusion and guilt developed over having to make that choice. From a position of security in their chosen category they could then find out about the other side of their heritage, and finally integrate both sides into their sense of self.

Since the late 1970s in the UK (Bagley and Young, 1979; Wilson, 1987), and the 1990s in the US (Root, 1996; Zack, 1995), studies of mixed race have tried to counter the idea that mixed race people suffer more than mono-heritage people from identity problems which are rooted in psychopathology or in dysfunctional family backgrounds. Studies found high levels of self-esteem amongst a sample of mixed race 4 to 7 year-olds (Bagley et al, 1979), and a small group of biracial adolescents (Gibbs and Hines, 1992). Self-identifying as mixed race was in itself an indicator of a positive identity for some researchers (Wilson, 1987; Tizard and Phoenix, 2001). Wilson (1987) found little evidence of identity confusion amongst a group of 9 year-olds. However, Wilson's assertion that most of the children in her study felt comfortable with what she calls an 'intermediate' mixed race identity was based on the participants having chosen a photograph of a child that looked most like them from a selection of photographs. This does not necessarily shed light on the positive or negative experience of being mixed race. Tizard and Phoenix (2001), with reference to research conducted with children in 1991, argued that positive racial identities were constructed in relation to racial norms, whereas identities formed when the children felt different, unhappy, confused about their identity or as if they did not 'belong' were deemed problematic identities (p108-109). Their assumption was that an individual's psychological health depended on her or his affiliation to an ethnic community.

Several British studies of children and young people of black and white parentage have revealed that mixed race people refer to themselves in terms of 'in between' categories, challenging the traditional idea that mixed race people are black or only have one racial identity. Wilson's study as early as 1987 showed that 59 per cent of 6 to 9 year-olds saw themselves as neither black or white but as 'brown', or 'half and half', 'coloured' or 'half-caste', whilst the study by Tizard and Phoenix (2001) showed that 49 per cent of respondents identified as 'mixed', 'brown', 'half and half', 'coloured' or 'half-caste' and 39 per cent as black. In other words mixed race people have increasingly identified as black and white, rather than black or white (Tizard and Phoenix, 2001; Rockquemore and Brunsma, 2002). Anzaldua (1987), in a US context, has des-cribed mixed race identity as a 'border identity', which lies in between two established social categories. In her opinion, mixed race people do not see themselves as either black or white but incorporate both black-ness and whiteness into a unique self-referential hybrid category.

The work of psychologists such as Erikson (1968) has been drawn on by some researchers in the UK and the US. Erikson claimed that many adolescents experienced an identity crisis in their bid to become 'inte-grated' adults. His developmental framework was used by Gibbs (1997) in her work with biracial adolescents to suggest that a biracial identity, not a black identity, was the desirable goal for mixed race people. How-ever, Gibbs reported that developmental problems could arise when mixed race adolescents experienced conflicts in their attempts to resolve basic psychosocial tasks. These problems included feelings of anxiety about social acceptance, shame about physical appearance, fear of rejection by peer groups and by one parental culture, difficulty in partnerships and anxiety over education and career options. Gibbs also argued that choosing the black culture over the white culture could re-sult in a negative identity formation which was associated with the de-valued social status of the black parent's culture. She pointed out that over-identification with the white parent as the symbol of the dominant culture could be at the expense of the minority culture.

In her study of mixed race children in Britain, Ali (2003) found that the identification of children with their parents occurred in the contexts of both gender and race and that understandings of race were closely con-nected to colour and appearance. Ali also observed that children with one black parent and one white parent sometimes identified as black but that none of the children with one parent from another ethnic minority culture ever identified solely with that culture.

The studies discussed in this section are interesting because they do not present mixed heritage identity as benign and unproblematic, as it is portrayed in much popular discourse. They reveal the ways in which mixed heritage subjectivities develop in relation to social and political factors such as social ascription, marginalisation and discrimination, and parents' heritages. This study does not delve into the psychological aspects of mixed heritage identity but draws on the existing studies to investigate social aspects of the women's identities.

Postmodernity and celebration: anything goes...

In the last decade there has been a growing body of work on critical mixed race theory, particularly in the US (Root, 1992, 1996; Zack, 1995; Daniel, 1996; Rockquemore and Brunsma, 2002; Mahtani, 2002; Winters *et al*, 2003), but also in the UK (Ifekwunigwe, 1999; Tizard and Phoenix, 2001; Alibhai-Brown, 2001; Parker and Song, 2001; Olumide, 2002; Ali, 2003; Ifekwunigwe, 2004). These studies have focused on mixed race people's own accounts and have opened up a theoretical space which is informed by their lived experiences. The idea that personhood is socially constructed, multiple and shifting has been helpful for understanding mixed race people's personal accounts and experiences (Anzaldua, 1987; Ahmed, 1997; Ifekwunigwe, 1999; Mahtani, 2002). It has challenged the view that mixed race people are black, and that mixed race identity is inherently problematic or patho-logical: it has focused instead on the heterogeneous nature of mixed heritage identity and the social processes involved in identity forma-tion.

Recent theoretical definitions of mixed race identity have broadened to encompass not only black and white heritage but dual or multiple ethnic minority heritage (Ifekwunigwe, 1999; Alibhai-Brown, 2001; Mahtani and Moreno, 2001; Olumide, 2002). These definitions reflect postmodern notions of identity as socially constructed, complex and contradictory. They have challenged reified and homogeneous notions of race, debunked the belief in racial purity (Ifekwunigwe, 1997), and confounded the idea that universal theories can be produced. The intersection between race, culture and other subjectivities such as class and gender has also been recognised (Anthias and Yuval-Davis, 1992; Reay, 1998; Ali, 2003).

Postmodern ideas around identity have been attractive to many researchers working in the field of the mixed race studies precisely be-cause they do not emphasise race and biology and encapsulate the diversity of mixed race identities. Expressions of contemporary mixed heritage identities may be based on race, culture, nationality, religion, country of birth or the environment in which a person was brought up.

39

The downside of this is that race is too readily conflated with culture. Culture is categorised as homogeneous and reified instead of race and becomes the dominant feature of identity (Rattansi, 1992; Gilroy, 2000). Within the context of multicultural Britain and increasing emphasis on political correctness around race, culture encompasses all elements of identity and difference. This over-usage of culture is most obvious in public discourse and is also often used in academic literature: we talk of multiculturalism, cultural groups, cultural difference, cultural diversity, cultural pluralism, and most recently cosmopolitanism, a nice clean term which has no suggestion of race embedded within it.

Because racism has become less focused on biology and more on cultural and other differences, complex and contradictory forms of discrimination have emerged. It has been suggested that a more nuanced notion of racism is required and that we should talk about 'racisms' to explain contemporary composite forms of discrimination (Goldberg, 1993; Back, 1994; Rattansi, 1995; Mac an Ghaill, 1999). One view is that because mixed race identity de-stabilises the homogeneity of fixed racial categorisations, it can be used as a potential antiracist strategy and lead the way towards a raceless future (Gordon, 1995). As mixed race people become more visible, attention is increasingly focused on them as harbingers of a more egalitarian and progressive society.

Postmodernist academic discourses around diversity are reflected in public and media discourses on mixed race. Mixed heritage people have always served some broader purpose in society to justify their existence: traditionally they were marginal and in the contemporary context they are embodiments of multiculturalism, bodies that are de-raced yet full of harmless culture. Laura Smith recently pointed out in *The Guardian* (2006): 'Suddenly our image is everywhere ... Mixed race people have become the acceptable face of ethnic minorities ... a handy shorthand for diversity without the potential alienation associated with using somebody too black, too different, too dangerous.' In Britain this 'commodification of otherness' (Razack, 1998, 5) has occurred at an unprecedented rate with mixed heritage celebrities but not in relation to black people. The danger of this celebration of mixed heritage is that it can lead to a fetishism of mixed heritage people in public and media discourse.

The established BBC internet site gives an insight into popular assumptions about mixed race people in Britain, and uses the race/culture conflation in a trouble-free manner. The opening article of Race UK, entitled 'The changing face of Britain: Britain's blurring ethnic mix', is an example of what Parker and Song (2001) refer to as the 'celebration' discourse of mixed race people as 'embodiments of the progressive and harmonious intermingling of cultures and people' and 'exemplars of contemporary cultural creativity' (p4). The leading caption, flanked by a photo of Dawn French and Lenny Henry, triumphantly claims: 'The United Kingdom has one of the fastest growing mixed race populations in the world, fuelled by the continuing rise of inter-ethnic relationships.' Shirley Bassey, Oona King MP and Hanif Kureshi are mentioned as high-profile examples of Britain's flourishing mixed heritage population. The article goes on to claim that 'Britons of all shades are embracing each other more than ever before' and informs us that celebrities such as Michael Caine and Trevor Macdonald, Sade and Salman Rushdie are, or have been, in mixed race relationships.

The article suggests that mixed race identity is no more than skin deep and that the primary indicator of a progressive multicultural and non-racist society is inter-racial marriage. Inter-racial relationships are described as a thriving industry, with a fifth of Asian men and 10 per cent of Asian women choosing a white partner. A much quoted statistic on mixed race relationships in recent years has been that 50 per cent of African Caribbean men and 30 per cent of African Caribbean women under the age of 30 who are partnered have white partners (Modood *et al*, 1997). Banks (2002), in a later study, quoted that 20 per cent of African Caribbean, 17 per cent of Chinese, and 4 per cent of Indian and African Asians had white partners. One entrenched stereotype about Asian people is that they tend to marry within their own ethnic group; the example of Asian/white inter-marriage might have been specifically chosen in this internet article to stress just how advanced British society is.

The question of feminism

This section addresses the issue of feminist politics and its relation to mixed race identity. To investigate this issue, the modernist versus post-modernist/post-structuralist debate, which spans western feminism, black feminism and feminism in critical mixed race studies, is discussed. This debate is fundamentally concerned with the materiality of the body. For mixed heritage women to be an effective political force, a mixed race category is prerequisite, and it must be clear who is in and out of this category.

Within academic discourse, race essentialist accounts of identity have largely been discounted in favour of a view of race as socially constructed. However, the debate between essentialism and social constructionism in the context of gender is still pertinent. Modernist western feminists such as Bordo (1989) have claimed that we need a unitary concept of womanhood within which to ground a feminist politics, and that the aim of politics should be to resist cultural constructions as they are presented to us (Assiter, 1996). Post-structuralist feminists such as Butler (1990) have asserted that the body – and so too womanhood – is an effect of discourse, a cultural sign from the outset, and that basing feminist politics on the materiality of the body is therefore misguided.

The main argument against the modernist position is that whilst modernist principles may be useful in providing a universal theory of equality and justice, a feminist epistemology based on a universal female identity is limited in that it draws on essentialist female values, and cannot give expression to all of women's experiences. It is therefore normative and exclusionary and cannot be in the interests of universal equality. The main argument against the post-structuralist position is that it is not able to sustain a unitary reform project precisely because it does not draw on a paradigm of universal femaleness (Hartsock, 1990; Soper, 1993). If the self as a unitary identity is deconstructed, it undermines the possibility of access to universal truth and experience, and if universal truths are ruled out then there can be no language of resistance (Lovibond, 1983; Cole and Hill, 1995). An emphasis on difference therefore leads to political ineffectiveness and dissipates the possibility for collective emancipatory action. Standpoint feminists have also criticised post-structuralism for being androcentric (Soper, 1993) and politically reactionary in its attempt to debilitate feminism's goals (Hartsock, 1990).

Whilst feminism in the 1980s focused on the right to be equal, the focus in the 1990s was on the right to be different and the endeavour by white feminists to try and compensate for their exclusionist politics. The reaction of black feminists to the politics of white feminists, and the inability of white feminism – which made specific claims around the family and the nature of patriarchy – to incorporate the experiences of black women, shifted the white feminist discourse from universalism to difference (Mirza, 1997). Black feminists increasingly demanded to be seen as culturally and not racially different (Anthias and Yuval-Davis, 1992). One of the dangers with universalist feminism was the assumption that all women were oppressed by patriarchy, whilst all black women were oppressed simultaneously by patriarchy, racial subordination, and the stigma of class (Carby, 1982, 213).

It was argued that not all black women experienced oppression in exactly the same way, and that there was a need 'to make a distinction between what it means to be from an oppressed group and yet be privileged – while still sharing in the collective reality of black women' (Childers and hooks, 1990, 75). The idea that the oppressed have a privileged position not only presupposes that there is a group of people who are fundamentally similar because of their sex or race, but also that women, unlike men, and black women, unlike white women, may be free of participation in relations of domination (Flax, 1990, 55-56).

White feminism could not resolve the problem of racial hegemony within gender relations. Its inclusive philosophy remained exclusive and inequitable in practice, and white feminists were unable to understand what it meant to be part of the dominant group (Frankenberg, 1993; Razack, 1998). Difference still privileged whiteness, and as difference was always perceived in relation to the white norm, white authority within the feminist movement was unavoidable. Within the academy the question of the legitimacy of standpoint feminism and its universalistic humanism weighed heavy for many black feminists whose voices could only be legitimated through white feminism (Ware, 1991; Mohanty, 2003).

During the 1990s there was a gradual shift in focus away from the body to political sites of struggle and exploring the ways in which the subject is constructed through social processes (Mouffe, 1995; Nicholson and Seidman, 1995; Ashenden, 1997). This came from the recognition that denouncing equality and justice in the name of difference would be a self-defeating and an unnecessary move, especially because the alternative would be a relativist politics which must ultimately condone a particularist deregulated social policy (Laclau and Mouffe, 1985; Benhabib and Cornell, 1987). Discarding the reified category woman did not necessarily lead to paralysis. It could open up new possibilities for feminism in organising feminist politics around particular identities, issues and struggles which had a broader democratic project in mind (Mouffe, 1995). From this perspective feminism could be seen as a 'permanently shifting political coalition', whereby identification with feminist struggles was not based on epistemology or fixed categories but on the problematic of social practices (Ashenden, 1997, 56) in which the subject was constituted through political identifications.

Mouffe's (1995) idea that fragmentation enables new constellations of unity in which political collectivities and coalitions are formed out of common interests which cut across specific identifications has been particularly useful for contemporary feminist philosophy. Mouffe (1995) argued that the feminist political movement should not be limited to pursuing feminist goals which only had the idea of 'women as women' in mind, but that it should be seen as a struggle against the plural forms in which the category woman is constructed in subordination, that is to say, through class, ethnicity and race. As Haraway (1990) has argued:

> There is nothing about 'female' that naturally binds women. There is not even such a state as 'being' female, itself a highly complex category constructed in contested sexual scientific discourses and other social practices. Gender, race, or class consciousness is an achievement forced on us by the terrible historical experience of the contradictory social realities of patriarchy, colonialism, racism and capitalism. (p197)

Several feminist theorists have attempted to reconfigure or marry elements of the modernist and postmodernist/post-structuralist positions in an attempt to show that a feminist project can be emancipatory and democratic without the category woman having a determinate meaning (Best and Kellner, 1997; Francis, 1999b). However, some post-structuralist feminist writers have pointed out that a combination of modernist and postmodernist principles may be not only theoretically dubious but empirically impracticable (Jones, 1997; Francis, 1999b). As such, the deconstructive dimension of postmodernism has been disregarded by many feminists because the preoccupation with difference and the denial of commonality leaves no theoretical or political tools for understanding how race, class and gender play out in people's lives, and for combating oppression (Hartsock, 1990).

One irony is that the modernist/post-structuralist debate within western feminist philosophy, and how to get round the problem of exclusion, was mirrored by the debate within black feminism in the 1990s. This debate focused on race, not womanhood, as the requisite social category for effective political action, and concerned the question of the materiality of blackness, as opposed to the materiality of the body (Butler, 1990, 1993). The main problem with this was who could, or should, be called black. The modernist discourse of blackness was an exclusionary one which could not account for differences within it; the postmodernist concept which embraced difference weakened the possibility of effective political action.

Parallel to the debate within the black feminist movement about who counts as black, is the question in critical mixed race theory about who counts as mixed race. Some academics, mainly in the US, have claimed that the political salience of the black movement is compromised if mixed race people do not define as black. One argument against a mixed race category has been that people who previously identified as black may defect to a mixed race grouping, which would undermine the universal antiracist political agenda (Gordon, 1995). Black and mixed race people should work together because they have common experiences of discrimination: separate identity claims of black and of mixed race people would make cohesive political action impossible. Prominent figures such as the late Bernie Grant, a black politician (*The Guardian*, 1997, 2), and media commentators such as Clare Gorham (*The Guardian*, 2003, 35) have underscored this view and expressed misgivings about a mixed race category. They have claimed that for political reasons, and because mixed race people encounter the same racism and discrimination as black people, it is imperative for mixed race people to identify as black.

Tessman (1999) has pointed out that there has been little consideration of a politics of racial self-identification which goes beyond essentialism and the idea of fitting in to a particular bounded identity. However, the heterogeneity of mixed race identities and experiences defies the emergence of a mixed race category. It is, as Ali (2003) has pointed out, 'the *inadequacy* of 'mixed race' as a single coherent category that makes it so theoretically demanding' (p5). Another difficulty with defining a category of mixed race for political purposes is that we cannot assume that all women who define as mixed race experience oppression in the same way. Nor can we assume that a majority mixed race group within an inclusive mixed race category would not emerge and silence the minority voices.

Ifekwunigwe (2001) has put forward a two-fold challenge: how to create an inclusive space for the formation of complex and multi-layered identities without resorting to either essentialist categories, or what Donovan Chamberlayne refers to as 'I am-ism' – 'I am not Black or White, I am just me' and how to forge political and social alliances from shared marginal status (p45). Razack (1998), although not referring specifically to mixed race identity, has claimed that it is important to move beyond essences but not simply to replace this with the assertion that we are all human beings.

The next three chapters examine the interview data on the women's perceptions of identity. They discussed how they understand the term mixed race, how they defined themselves, their experiences of adapting in different contexts and how they had changed over time or in response to some turning point in their lives. They described how they felt they were seen by other people and their experiences of difference and discrimination. The data reveal that the women drew on discourses of cultural diversity and race essentialism to talk about their own identities and experiences. Race was not an unpalatable aspect of identity as much of the academic and policy literature suggests. On the contrary, it was intrinsic to conceptions of selfhood, relationships, and experiences of categorisation and discrimination.

3

Constructing selfhood

This chapter explores how the women defined mixed race, and how they defined themselves. It also examines what they said about their experiences of adapting in different situations, and how they felt they had changed over time or due to a turning point or major event in their lives. The women drew on an array of discourses in their constructions of identity, and the theories and discourses about mixed heritage which have already been discussed are used to illuminate these discourses. In discussing the data, the basic premise is that knowledge is historically and culturally specific and that identities are socially constructed through language (Foucault, 1972, 1979). The words presented here are not representative of who the respondents are or what they believe, but reflect their versions of reality at given moments. We cannot deduce from the women's talk exactly what they meant by what they said, and whether they engaged analytically with the discourses they drew on: their talk about race essentialism or diversity simply reflected a race essentialist or postmodernist discourse.

Understandings of mixed race

The interviewees were asked: *What does the term mixed race mean to you?* Just under half the women had a dual concept of race and used the words 'two' or 'half' in terms of races, heritages and to describe mixed race identity. Only two of the women who had a dual concept of race specifically said that being mixed race meant having one black and one white parent, whilst the others all said that it could be a combination of any two races. Corinna (Jamaican/Irish) said:

> Mixed race is some kind of black and some kind of white – Indian and white, Chinese and white, Indian and Chinese, but Indian and black is coolie.

The finding reflects the general shift away from the black/white binary model towards a more pluralistic concept of mixed race which incorporates ethnic minority/white and dual ethnic minority heritage (Ifekwunigwe, 1999; Mahtani and Moreno, 2001; Alibhai-Brown, 2001; Olumide, 2002).

Just over half of the women used the words 'mixture' or 'different' to describe mixed race heritage, where this mixture could refer to races, cultures, nationalities and religions. These women used what could be called a diverse concept of mixed race, in which more than two heritages could constitute mixed race identity. Notions of diversity included second generation and multiple heritage, and intra-continental heritage and/or dual ethnic minority heritage.

Many of the women talked about mixed race as being about race and culture, including the five respondents who described their mixed race as intra-continental. For Ella (Burmese/Mauritian) and Soraya (English/Turkish), the issue of race became confused with culture, and concepts such as country, language and religion became aspects of race or culture. As they talked, they became uncertain about what they meant by the terms they were using. Ella said:

> It's got nothing to do with culture, if you're from two countries in Asia you're one race, and from one country in Africa and one in Asia then you're mixed race. But Caribbean and African is also mixed race, and Chinese and Indian, I don't know why.

For Soraya, being mixed race could mean coming from different continental regions, religions, languages and traditions, or the way someone looked:

> [Mixed race means] ... coming from two different races. Mediterranean – Spain, Greece, Turkey – is a race separate from European. Part of what comes into your race is your religion, like Pakistani and Indian are different races. Cypriot-Turks and Cypriot-Greeks consider themselves different from mainland Turks or Greeks – they speak each other's language, and the traditions are identical, but a Greek is a Greek and a Turk

is a Turk. I can tell Greeks and Turks apart. Germans and English are a different race because they look different – I can tell a German a mile away. I think it's the self-definition that counts.

Paula (Rumanian/Greek), whose parents had different cultures and practiced different religions, had grown up believing her parents also came from different races '*because my mum was very, very dark and my dad white, and my mum did things one way and my dad another*'.

In describing what mixed race meant to them, all the second generation and multiple heritage women referred to a mixture of races, as opposed to cultures or nationalities, to describe mixed race identity. Nichole, who described herself as three quarters Black and a quarter White, and Peta, who described herself as African and West Indian-English, both asserted that mixed race was '*not being 100 per cent one thing*'. This statement supports the idea that pure races exist, and that one drop of blood, as in hypodescent (Root, 1996), is enough to alter a person's racial category. Rosa (Angolan-Portuguese/Portuguese) drew on essentialist notions of race, and suggested that there were many different races:

> [Mixed race is] ... people of different races – there's Asian, that's one race from the Indian continent, and another is Oriental, European, South American, White, Eskimos and Siberians...

Although not specifically asked about ethnic monitoring, several women stated that they disliked it, and that it was discriminatory. Anabel (Guyanese/Indian-White) said:

> It was only when I came out here, after filling in these forms and they ask you about ethnic background, that is when I realised how much, how big an issue it actually is, this whole question of identity ... it's really baffling, this differentiation between people.

Kim (African [Cuban-Jamaican]/English) regarded the '*simple fact that you have to state your race*' as a form of racism because she believed that ethnic monitoring information was not used in ways which benefited ethnic minority people, and that there was no evidence of increasing racial equality. Nadine (Iraqi/English) rejected this form of classification because she believed that employers could not be trusted not to discriminate against people on the grounds of race, sex and age:

It gets ridiculous with these forms – sometimes I say 'mixed race' under 'other' and sometimes I just say oh none of your business – what's the point, why are you asking these questions, it sort of seems racist in a way even making it an issue. It's a bit like when you send an application form off for a job – wouldn't it be much better if they didn't know how old you were, what sex you were, or what race you were or anything, you know, that you're just a name?

There are two main points about the findings in this section and how they relate to the broader theoretical and discursive issues discussed in Chapter Two. Concepts of mixed race identities as socially hetero-geneous indicated a lack of satisfaction with dualistic explanations of mixed race identity (Bhabha, 1990; Hall, 1992). These concepts did not fit with a definitive category of mixed race in which people identify with a black/white binary model (Tizard and Phoenix, 2001; Wilson, 1987), or a dual or diverse ethnic minority model (Ifekwunigwe, 1999; Mahtani and Moreno, 2001; Alibhai-Brown, 2001; Olumide, 2002). Also, despite the ease with which many of the women talked about mixed race identity as diverse, they still viewed races, cultures, religions and national identities as distinct entities. Soraya (English/Turkish) main-tained that Germans were a separate race from English people – as if each race possessed distinctive characteristics. Therefore, even when concepts of mixed race identity were taken to postmodern extremes in terms of the type and quantity of specific heritages possible in a person, it was a discourse of postmodernism based on fixed race essentialist categories.

Defining the self: '*I feel like a person, not more white or more black, just mixed*'

The rejection of the traditional binary concept of mixed race, and the postmodern idea that personhood is fluid and multiple was also re-flected in the women's self-conceptions of mixed race. They often meticulously recounted their multiple heritages, including those of their grandparents and great-grandparents. As such, mixed race identity was conceptualised as additive in that over generations more and more races could exist in one person.

Daniel (1996) has argued that a mixed heritage person who possesses a pluralistic (meaning neither black, white nor biracial) and an integrative (the blending of black and white) identity may produce a sense of selfhood which transcends race. Rockquemore and Brunsma (2002) have also referred to a transcendent identity to describe respondents in their study who 'opt[ed] out of the categorisation game altogether' (p50), and were able to be objective about the social meaning of race, and discount its 'master status' (p51). The perspectives of Daniel (1996) and Rockquemore and Brunsma (2002) suggest that mixed heritage people can pursue identities which are outside the realm of race. Their research was based largely on people of American African/European American descent, and sheds little light on other mixed heritage experiences. Nevertheless, these authors' views are supported by my research in that most of the women conceptualised mixed heritage as pluralistic, and explicitly rejected categorisation on the lines of race and colour and viewed themselves as unique individuals. However, they did not see themselves as transcending race in that race was also a fundamental aspect of selfhood.

The women were asked the question: *What is important to you in how you define who you are?* The most frequent responses were *'being mixed race'* or *'mixedness'* and *'personality'*. Interestingly, almost half the women's immediate first response to the question was *'not by race'* or *'not by colour'*. Adriana (Angolan-Portuguese/Angolan) said vehemently:

Not by the colour of my skin at all, never, how I am, how I present myself, how I interact with other people. It's a matter of common sense, not looking at someone, like they say, not looking at the book and judging it by the cover.

Most of the women who rejected self-definition based on race and colour said that their personality was the most important factor in defining themselves. Typical responses were that they wanted to be seen *'just as me'*, *'just as a person'*, *'for the person within'*, *'as an individual'*, *'as a unique person'*, or *'as a human being'*. Dianne (Welsh/Mauritian) said:

My race is how people see me first, that's how they build a foundation and they elaborate from there. I don't see that race should be an issue – it's not an issue for me and it's not an issue amongst my friends. Your identity expresses who you are as a person – it's very important to just be yourself.

Four people also said that religion was important in how they defined themselves, four said '*what I do*', two said '*knowledge*', and one, Anabel (Guyanese/Indian-White), said:

> As a human being. Personally I dislike it when people say I'm black, because I will tell them if you look at my bag, that's black, I'm not black. To be honest, I'm not too keen about this issue of race and colour, I just view myself as a professional woman ...

The notion of personality was often juxtaposed with being mixed race, as in 'I am me, I am mixed race'. Respondents wanted to be seen by others as unique individuals, where being valued as mixed race was intrinsic to that uniqueness. In just a few words Jennifer (Caribbean-Portuguese-Asian/English-Irish) communicated the ambiguity she felt around defining and presenting herself as mixed, and in terms of her personality:

> Mixedness is not important in how I define who I am, although I want to put it across. My personality is important. I feel like a person, not more white or more black, just mixed.

Danielle (Jamaican/English) asserted that how she put herself across was more important than being mixed race, because mixed race identity was a kind of no-man's-land, a state of '*not really being anything*' and '*not having a culture*'. Danielle described being mixed race as

> ... not having a race to fall back on, because most people are either black or white and it's sort of like being in the middle and not really being anything, because mixed race can be anything, it's not determined by a certain race, just sort of in between ... What is important to me is just getting myself across and letting people know what I am and what I stand for.

Although so many of the women spurned classifications based on race or colour, many also drew on race to describe themselves. Nearly all the first generation black/white women specifically stated that being mixed race was important to them and that they wanted both their black and white sides to be recognised. Lesley (Bajan/Scottish), for example, said that it was important to recognise both heritages of mixed race people:

> Mixed race is very, very important because a lot of white people see only the black in you and the same with black people, they see only the white. That way one side is always denied.

Corinna (Jamaican/Irish) felt irritated about having to classify herself as other, and was adamant that she wanted to be recognised as mixed race:

> As I got older, especially when I fill out application forms, some of them have the mixed race box and some of them don't, so you have to put 'other' and write it in, and I think as I've got older and I've seen them little things it's made me change as I want to be recognised as mixed race because it's what I am. I don't want to be classed as 'other', somebody who's not recognised. I'm not black, I'm not white, I'm mixed race.

Notably, all the second generation respondents vehemently rejected ascription, and although all identified as mixed race, they also identified with their black heritage. This correlates with the study by Tizard and Phoenix (2001) which showed that 39 per cent of the mixed race children identified as black, and is not surprising given the findings in Fatimilehin's (1999) study which showed that whilst many respondents identified as mixed race, even more identified as mono-racially black. Peta (African/West Indian-English), who asserted '*I'm white and I'm black*', described her culture as '*very English*', and also believed that her individuality was strongly connected to her African heritage:

> I don't look at the colour of my skin, colour doesn't come into it – I am me, I am unique and there's nobody else like me. I'm more black African than anything else, who you mix with doesn't influence how you feel inside. If people ask me I'm African, I've got the strongest roots there ... I was closest to dad, which has influenced the way I see myself. I wanted to be like him, so if that meant I had to eat rice then I would do that. Now I cook African food, have pictures on the wall, watch documentaries on Africa.

Many of the women emphasised their parents' heritages, and in some cases their grandparents' heritages, in describing their mixed identity. Therefore 'who I am' was understood as 'who I am a part of' and 'where I come from', as can also be seen in Peta's quote above. The following quotes illustrate this point:

> When people bring it up I have to make sure they know I'm black and white. If people say 'are you black?' I say no, I'm both, my mum's in the picture. I feel mixed race because of the colour of my skin, that's the main

reason. And because of my father. I've got to admit he's still there – he brought me into this world, so I can't just say I'm white, I couldn't do that, I don't think it would be right, denying part of my family. Lianne (St. Lucian/English)

Because that's where my mum's from and I'm part of my mum ... it's important, and you know you're from there, so you got to take an insight into what kind of things they do, you can't forget about something that is part of you. Petra (African/Portuguese)

It is important to be aware of your roots, your culture, where you're from ... I think you should never forget your origins in a way. It should be a strong part of you because that's where you're from. It's a part of my identity, part of me. Ella (Burmese/Mauritian)

This finding is consistent with how many of the women were precise about their exact racial mix, tracing it back to parents, grandparents, and even great grandparents in descriptions of their mixed heritage identity. This is interesting because two-thirds of the women were brought up in mono-heritage households, and their other heritage was often marginal or completely absent from their lives. This theme is explored further in Chapter Five.

Three points can be made so far:

- ■ Many women denounced racial ascription, yet used the concept of race to describe themselves, and being mixed race was seen by nearly all first generation black/white women as central to their sense of self.

- ■ Nearly half the sample viewed their personality as the most important aspect of their identity, and for many being mixed race was an intrinsic part of their personality.

- ■ Many women talked about their mixed heritage identity as inextricably linked to their parents' racial and cultural heritages.

On friendship: 'Black people, they're my own kind. White is my own kind as well ...'

The findings on friendship gave an indication about who the women identified with. The question asked was: *Are you drawn to particular groups of people – who are your friends?* Only two women said they were more drawn to white people, which is surprising given that most of the women grew up in predominantly white home environments. The responses from all the other women to some extent reflected a diverse concept of friendship. Whilst over half the sample evoked an inclusive postmodern discourse and claimed that race and colour were unimportant, a substantial number of women specifically excluded white people from descriptions of their friendships.

Twenty two women reflected the diversity concept of friendship and said they were drawn to people and had friends from a variety of backgrounds, mentioning any combination of established categories such as black, white and Asian. Many of them distinguished between race and personality in describing their friendships. Cassandra (Jamaican/ Irish) said: *'People I get along with I get along with no matter what colour or race they are. It just depends on the person itself.'*

Sixteen women drew on a 'limited diversity' discourse of friendship and said they were drawn to either black, ethnic minority or mixed race people, or a combination of these. Three respondents, Anisha, Jasmine and Kerry, specifically said they were drawn mainly to mixed race people. Anisha (Indian/white American) was drawn to Indian/white mixed race people because of shared cultural similarities:

> I've developed friendships with a few people in my life who happen to be half-white half-Indian, and I don't mean happen to be, because I think there is a reason, I think that that was the bonding point. I understand what it's like to have different worlds, and one thing I do understand about that is that if you are mixed you are in this place that's in between.

Danielle, whose father was English and mother Jamaican, said she identified most with Asian culture, especially Islam and Hinduism. Dianne's (Welsh/Mauritian) comments reflected the stereotype that ethnic minority people are seen to have culture and white people are not:

> I get on more with ethnic minorities, mainly Mauritians, and Nigerians as well, because they have more culture to relate to like food ... English people don't tend to have a culture, they don't have values, they've only got Sunday lunch.

Ruby (Punjabi Indian/Irish) talked about a 'newer community' made up of mixed race and other marginalised people, to which she felt she belonged:

> Most people I feel really close to have felt marginalised or excluded from their own communities, and in a way I feel part of the 'newer community' because of that. Quite a lot of these people are mixed race. We do gravitate towards each other which isn't random, is more than just luck. I think it's often because I find myself in places searching for things at the same time as other people.

In the section on self-definition we saw how many first generation women asserted both the black and white sides of their heritage. In their constructions of self, they appeared to be separating themselves from, and indeed defending themselves against, the idea that racial homogeneity could be impressed upon them from outside. In articulations around friendship, a few women evoked homogenous race categories, in which they distinguished between themselves as mixed race, and black or white others. In so doing, they made an association between race and personality/behaviour. This kind of link can be seen in traditional psychology, which uses a common sense notion of personality that can be described as essentialist in so far as it makes a direct link between personality and behaviour (Burr, 1995, 19).

In the quotes below, and other discussions about the race/personality theme, it is important to remember that essentialist thinking is constructed, and that in drawing on a race/personality discourse, the women's views reflected popular social constructions around identity. This analysis therefore does not contradict the theoretical position which views race and race thinking as socially constructed. Moreover, it cannot be assumed that the women were unaware of, or did not critically engage with, how race categories were constructed, and how the people they talked about were positioned by discourse. This study focuses primarily on how discourses were reflected in the women's talk: what they meant by what they said is beyond the scope of this analysis.

Lekeisha, who described herself as 'fully mixed Jamaican', constituting Indian, Chinese and Turkish heritage, distinguished between the supposed personality differences between black and white girls, and rejected what she saw as the negative black personality traits in herself and other black people. She chose not to associate with black girls because of their discriminatory attitudes towards white people, and with white girls because of their 'barbie-ness', in favour of a racially mixed group of boys who just had fun. For Lekeisha, the gender specific racial diversity of a group of boys, in which everyone was understood to be the same regardless of race or colour, formed a protection against racism. To her, a group of racially mixed girls was less appealing:

> To be honest I hardly ever hang around with black girls cos there's something, I just don't like their attitude. I do have a temper and everything, but certain things they do I don't agree, like most things they do I don't like, their racist comments about white people or mixed people and that. The white girls I hang around with have been called things you wouldn't like to hear, and they know what it's like. It's their personality, it's about personality – some white girls I won't hang around with because it's too like a Barbie, too much like a Barbie, so I'm like you're not my type of person. Like it depends on the person itself. Black girls I'd call more like a tomboy, more like a tomboy than a Barbie.

> Mainly I hang around with boys, and it's just like, I find it so much fun! It's like when I go out with a group of them it has to be mixed. So you know when you're in a group and someone passes a racist comment, it affects all of us not just one, cos in a way we're all different, and it's not about your culture.

Little reference was made to gender in the interviews generally, although a few women alluded to gender differences relating to attitudes to education and bullying. This supports the post-feminist discourse (see Whelelan, 1995; Volman and Ten Dam, 1998; McRobbie, 2000) in which any notion of gender inequality is regarded as outdated and insignificant. Race was the focus in my conversations with the women. As Lekeisha's talk illuminates, constructions of racial identity were clearly gendered: she made a distinction between gender difference and other kinds of difference. Ironically, whilst allegiance within such a group was forming a protection against racism, it was gender exclusive. Lekeisha distanced herself from what she saw as negative female traits and from any idea of female solidarity, and aligned herself firmly with the boys. She created a tomboy/Barbie dualism in her description of the difference between white girls and black: white girls displayed more feminine traits, in so far as Barbie represents the archetypal feminine woman, whilst black girls expressed themselves in tomboy and more masculine ways. Therefore, whereas being mixed and different had positive and transformative potential in that it could ultimately challenge racism, difference and the transgression of norms of gendered behaviour were seen as problematic.

Interestingly, this perceived masculinity in black girls was associated with a type of *'personality'*, *'attitude'*, *'temper'*, and *'racist comments'*, yet Lekeisha did not represent the boys as expressing these characteristics. She framed herself within a specific version of femininity which rejects what she saw as female expressions of masculinity or excessive femininity. In this sense she can be seen as constructing a 'middle position' on gender. The behavioural constraints caused by her pathologisation of representations of gender among her female contemporaries show some of the tensions and psychic costs of maintaining this position.

Like Lekeisha, Cerisse's (Scottish-African/Zambian-English) talk underscored the ways in which black girls are masculinised and pathologised in discourse: *'Most of the black girls here have attitude, some are aggressive and go round in gangs. I just keep myself to myself and don't get in anyone's way.'* All the respondents who mentioned boyfriends and dating said they preferred black men, again linking race to an essential notion of personhood or physical type.

Both Charmaine (Jamaican/White), and Lesley (Bajan/Scottish) drew on a race/behaviour/personality correlate in their representations of black and white people. For Charmaine, negotiations around her own identity rested on what she referred to as black and white *'kinds'*:

> Black people ... they're my own kind. White is my own kind as well, but I'm more on the black side. I get along with them more better. I've always been more around black people, but I don't act black, most people say I act white. I like white people, yeah, I don't mind them but, I just get on by my own tack but, well, I'm half and half, so I get on more with black people, I don't know why.

Lesley's talk highlights some of the complex issues around negotiating identity and friendship. Lesley's best friend was white – *'She always hangs around with us, she fits in, she's one of us'* – and yet Lesley said that she herself '*felt out of place around white people*' and was drawn mainly to black people. At the same time, she did not see herself as possessing distinctively black personality traits, and was '*quieter and more self-conscious around black girls cos black people are a lot ruder than white people, a lot ruder, and I'm not like that, I'm not a rude person.*' Lesley's suggestion was that black and white social groups displayed distinctive types of behaviour, but that racial boundaries were fuzzy enough to allow people, such as her friend, to move across them as long as they fitted in. In the next section, the theme of adapting is examined.

Adapting: '*I'm a bit of everything, so I don't just act in one way*'

The next question was designed to find out about being mixed race as a state of in-betweenness (Anzaldua, 1987; Wilson, 1987; Tizard and Phoenix, 2001). It asked: *Do you feel that you adapt in, or to, different cultural situations?* The aim was to see whether the women felt that they behaved differently in different racial or cultural settings. The women were being asked whether they felt that they possessed different personality traits which correlated with their different racial or cultural heritages, and which surfaced in different situations. Notions of 'integrative identities' (Daniel, 1996) and 'fluid identities' (Root cited in Rockquemore and Brunsma, 2002, 48) are useful for framing this question. Daniel has distinguished between a synthesised integrative identity, in which people feel equally comfortable in black and white locations, and a functional integrative identity, in which mixed heritage people function in both communities, but feel a stronger identification with either black or white people. Root has pointed out that the mixed heritage person has the ability to alternate between identities: to be black, white or mixed race in different situations.

I also wanted to find out whether the women felt marginal or out of place, and to follow up Gibbs's (1997) observations that mixed race people may experience feelings of anxiety about social acceptance and fear rejection by peer groups or one parental culture. These issues are also discussed in the next two chapters on experiences of categorisation and discrimination, and personal evolutions.

More than half the women said that they did adapt themselves to different cultural situations, whilst just over a third said that they did not. Those who did not adapt tended to focus on personality, where this was an unchanging facet of personhood. Responses such as '*I am who I am, it doesn't matter who I am with*', '*my personality always stays the same*', and '*I think I am always myself*' were typical. Nalia (three quarters Black/a quarter Chinese) said: '*If there was a group of all different races I don't think I would be more inclined to go over to the black people or not. I would say from past experience it's more the person.*' Lianne was vehement in her assertion that she did not adapt:

> No, not at all. It's just me. I can't explain it but I don't feel that at all, I don't feel more one way when I'm in a different situation, I just feel myself, just the same person. I don't change, I don't do things differently with other people.

Most of the women who said they did adapt in different cultural settings tended to refer to identity as 'fluid', in the sense that Root (cited in Rockquemore and Brunsma, 2002, 48) suggested. Some said they '*put on an act*', talking about different things or behaving in different ways, when they were with people from their minority heritage. Sherry (Guyanese/German) said:

> It's funny how you slip into the way they [black relatives] talk, the patterns and intonations, and then when you leave you become all English again! I try not to do it, but it comes out.

Ruby (Punjabi Indian/Irish), who had been adopted by white parents, talked about how her early experiences of having to adapt herself to a white environment had meant that adapting had become a way of life for her:

> I did this as a survival technique from an early age, and part of what's important in my development is rejecting that. I really check myself now, I still do it, but am much more aware of what I'm doing and why, and I really question myself and it's really hard work.

Notably, the three respondents who were most drawn to mixed race people said that they adapted to different situations but that mixed race people were the only people they did not adapt with. Jasmine (Grenadian-Scottish/Dominican) said she often changed around black people because she wanted to be accepted by them, but with mixed race people she was '*just myself.*' Anisha (Indian/white American), who '*playact[ed] Indianness*', felt that she could be freer with mixed race people than with either Indian or white people because of the likelihood of some resonance with them. Kerry (English/Bajan), who talked extensively about her experiences of being bullied and racially abused by black people at school, said that she was '*totally different around people of different races*'. On being with mixed race people, however, she said: '*Then I'm just me cos I know they're just being them and I can say whatever I like.*'

Some women separated what they saw as their core unchanging personality from the part of their identities which adapted in different settings. Frida (Colombian/Polish Jewish-English) said that putting on an act was a necessary part of everyday life, and she showed different sides of her personality because '*there's definitely certain behaviour, certain ways of speaking that in certain environments just don't make sense, and it's not a big deal.*' At the same time she did not '*feel any different inside*' and did not adapt '*in a way that is compromising or that I'm insincere or lose my integrity.*' Frida therefore talked about the difference between behaviour – what people do in different situations – and personality – what people feel in different situations. Chantel (English/African) also said that she did not think her personality changed at all, but that her behaviour was slightly different around African or English people: '*I think I'm a bit of everything, so I don't just act in one way.*' Similarly, Brenda (Afro-Caribbean/Indian-white Jewish) said that she very much remained herself in different cultural settings – '*I am what I am*' – but that she changed around African people – '*I know how far I can go with them culturally.*'

Jennifer drew on the race/personality association in her claim that her personality did not change in different cultural situations – '*Some people are affected by race and colour and how they act around them, but I'm just the same*', yet also said that she changed around black people, and that this was '*because of their personality, not their race.*'

Some women felt considerable pressure from people who adhered to fixed notions about what they believed constituted black or ethnic minority communities, and impressed these views on them. Nadine (Iraqi/English) felt awkward around Muslims because she felt they expected her to behave in a certain way, and she constantly tried to find a balance between adapting to her father's culture and rejecting the aspects that she did not agree with. Ruby (Punjabi Indian/Irish) said that she was resigned to Indian people expecting her to know things about Indian culture – '*It makes me feel frustrated, and a bit sad. I used to be angry about it, but I'm a bit weary about it now.*' Lekeisha, who had been brought up as Jamaican in England, felt that when she was with her mother she had to deny the part of herself that was English:

> My mum doesn't even understand me when I speak – she tells me I'm speaking too much English, stop it! Yes, I get pissed off when she doesn't understand me, what I'm saying, cos in a way I do have more Jamaican stuff on me, but I don't feel I'm more Jamaican than anything else.

Being able to adapt was seen as a positive attribute by some women. Corinna (Jamaican/Irish) evoked the celebratory discourses of multi-culturalism and mixed race in that she felt that being mixed race gave her the opportunity to see and understand more about the world, which in turn made her more open-minded:

> I can get on with anybody. At home I live in a white culture, and then at my father's house I'm living around a black culture, so I'm seeing two worlds, two cultures, two sets of people ... so I know how to get along with white people very well and I know how to get along with black people very well, so I think it's broadened my mind to just getting along with people as a whole.

This chapter has shown how discourses around race, diversity and individuality were embedded in the women's talk, and sat comfortably side by side. Most significantly, there was a conceptual paradox around race: many women readily dismissed the concept of race in self-definitions, and in talk about friendship and adapting in different situations. Yet they also saw race as significant in their assertions of mixed race self-hood, in describing their friendships, and in constructing identity in opposition to homogeneously perceived others, in which a person's race is linked to a certain kind of behaviour or personality. These apparently contradictory findings correlate with the equally contradictory popular discourses which exist around race essentialism, postmodern diversity and race invisibility.

4

The perceptions of others

C hapter Three examined some aspects of how the women defined and perceived themselves. This chapter looks at how they
believed they were perceived and treated by others. The issue is
significant in the context of this study because of the ambiguous ways
in which mixed heritage is constructed by discourse. Postmodern
theory, the celebratory discourse of mixed heritage, and the idea that
race is not an issue, suggest that the women may not have negative experiences *vis-á-vis* their mixed heritage identity. The persistence of race
essentialist discourse and race inequalities in society, however, indicate
that they may.

Most of the research on identity presumes the interrelationship
between subject and society, in which individuals are situated within
social environments that designate available categories of identification and set limits on how people are able to understand themselves.
Self-perceptions of identity are not constituted in a vacuum but are
socially constructed in specific contexts. According to Nagel (1996) a
person's ethnic identity is a mixture of subjectivity and ascription:

> An individual's ethnic identity is a composite of the view one has of
> oneself and the opinions held by others about one's ethnicity. The
> result is a volitional, if circumscribed model of ethnicity. Ethnic identity
> lies at the intersection of individual ethnic self-definition (who I am)
> and collective ethnic attribution (who they say I am). Ethnic identity is
> then a dialectic between internal identification and external
> ascription. (p21)

Rockquemore and Brunsma's (2002) notion of validated and un-validated identities is usefully applied to how the women in my study thought they were perceived by others. Border identities such as mixed race are validated within the interactional sphere and can acquire social meaning where self-perceptions and social ascriptions are in accordance:

> If identity is perceived as an interactionally validated self-understanding, then identities can only function effectively where the response of individuals to themselves (as social objects) is consistent with the response of others. In this schema, individuals cannot effectively possess an identity that is not socially typified; there must be no disjuncture between the identity actors appropriate for themselves and the place others assign to them as a social object. (Rockquemore and Brunsma, 2002, 41)

Identities that are not validated occur when racial self-understanding does not match the identity ascribed by others. Rockquemore and Brunsma (2002) state:

> Unvalidated border individuals also consider themselves to be uniquely biracial; however, their program is not validated. Others primarily assume they are black, and therefore, they report experiencing the world as a black person, although they understand themselves as a biracial person. When people's racial program is not validated by others in their significant social network, they either alter their program or remain in a nebulous, marginal and unresolved state with regard to their racial identity. (p93)

Some studies have found that the relationship between appearance and racial identification is significant, whereas others have found that the relevance of appearance has been eclipsed by social factors. In contrast to Rockquemore and Brunsma's (2002) study, which showed that there was a link between the women's self-perceptions and how they believed they were seen by others (p91), my study showed a discrepancy between self-perception as mixed race and how respondents believed they were seen by others as either black or mono-racial.

On categorisation
Perceptions of others: '*It's just I wanna be called what I am*'

The question asked was: *How do you think people you don't know see you?* It was carefully worded to get the women to think about how strangers perceived them in formal settings, as opposed to how they thought they were seen by friends. None of the respondents reported that they felt that they were seen for their personalities or for who they really are, which is surprising when well over half the sample said that their personality was important in how they defined themselves.

The way the women thought they were seen by others correlated with the way they perceived themselves in only seven cases. These seven were correctly categorised: the women, all first generation, said they were '*probably*', '*mostly*', or '*always*' seen as mixed race. Corinna (Jamaican/Irish), describing how she thought other people saw her, said:

> As mixed race and I hope to think as lucky. I've got the best of both worlds, so I've never really yeah had, nobody's ever really said anything to me, so I don't really know what people's opinions are, I just hope they see me as mixed race and lucky.

Despite being correctly categorised as mixed race, a number of women experienced this as negative. Danielle (English/Jamaican) felt annoyed that people did not look beyond race, and constantly compared her with mixed heritage celebrities because she had curly hair:

> A few people say racist things, like there's only a few famous people are mixed race, and people come up and say I look like Mel B or Alicia Keys – just cos I've got curly hair people think I look like Mel B – and I find it really annoying and derogatory. I felt it was robbing me of my identity, and it has influenced the way I look at the way people use race to determine who people are. It has made me think that we shouldn't use race to determine how people should be.

Kerry (English/Bajan) was often asked which parent was black and which parent was white:

> They [people] are always shocked when I say that my mum's black and my dad's white, they always assume that it's the other way round. But once they've got past that they don't normally ask any more questions. It

did used to annoy me when I was younger, I used to feel I should walk around with a sign on my head saying 'my mum's black and my dad's white', but now I've got used to it.

Just under three quarters of the sample (29) said that other people saw them as mono and not mixed heritage. These are incorrect categorisations. The findings show a remarkable disjuncture between perceptions of self as mixed race and how the women felt they were perceived by others as mono-racial. In this sense these women possessed what Rockquemore and Brunsma (2002) referred to as an unvalidated identity. This finding echoes Mahtani and Moreno's (2001) assertion that mixed race people have been made intelligible in ways that maintain racial differentiation and hierarchies in that they have been categorised as either black or white. The fact that they have been forced to choose one identity, usually the minority identity, has resulted from the legacy of hypodescent (Root, 1996; Alibhai-Brown, 2001). Hypo in this case meant lower or under, and hypodescent meant that the mixed heritage person would take on the identity of the racial group that was designated lower status.

It is, however, unclear whether the women's experiences of miscategorisation meant that they thought that people did not physically recognise them as mixed heritage, or whether, as Mahtani and Moreno (2001) and others have pointed out, mixed heritage is simply not recognised as a valid identity. Omi and Winant (1994) have described the encounter with the mixed heritage person as the moment of 'crisis of racial meaning' (p59), in which a separation between, and negotiation around, existing categories of race and the person who does not fit these categories occurs. Despite new heterogeneous constructions of personhood, there is still an enduring expectation that people are mono-racial: this is compulsory mono-raciality, in which homogenous discourses around race/culture/ethnicity remain dominant.

Out of the 29 women who thought they had been incorrectly categorised, 21 were first generation mixed heritage, and eight were second generation or multiple heritage. Their responses fall into three groups.

1. Eight first generation mixed race women thought that they were classified in mono-heritage terms and ascribed a racial heritage, such as black or Asian, which corresponded broadly with one of their

parents' heritages. The persistence of race essentialist views, and the assumptions made about the women based on their perceived race, are shown in the comments made by Lianne and Tania:

> Even though I look mixed race, a lot of people see me as black and expect me to act and be a certain way. So I have to put the point across that I am mixed race. Black boys often say, oh, you must like this or like that because you're black. Lianne (St. Lucian/English)

> I think people see me as black, not mixed, but when they get to know me I'm probably very white. I don't think it enters people's minds that my husband might be white, they just see me with a black man. Even now people are surprised when they see my husband, and my kids. Tania (West Indian/English)

Amongst this group of women, some felt that they were seen as black, but at the same time as not black enough. They felt discriminated against, and in a no-win situation.

2. One quarter of the sample said that people tended to assume that they had mono-heritage backgrounds which did not correspond with either of the women's parental heritages. Some respondents in this group said they disliked other people's wrong assumptions about them, whilst others talked about the funny side of people's mis-constructions.

Nadine (Iraqi/English) thought that she was seen as *'European or French or something'* and added *'these days it's okay to be French, isn't it?'* Nadine also said that she was

> cagey about her background because there's a lot of animosity and that can be quite difficult. People don't understand the difference between being pro-Iraqi and pro-Saddam Hussein.

Tasha (black American/English) was frequently asked if she was Chinese, whilst Frida (Colombian/Polish Jewish-English) felt that she was incorrectly labelled as Pakistani. Her views on this are discussed in the next chapter.

Anita's (Mauritian/Filipino) comments can be understood as a double misconstruction of her racial heritage. People would often assume that she was South Asian, and after being told her actual heritage, would think that she should look Chinese:

> Everyone thinks I'm Indian or Bangladeshi. I think it's funny cos when I then tell people what I am they get so shocked and say I don't look Chinese at all!

Dianne (Welsh/Mauritian) talked about the manifold racial identities other people assigned to her, and how she dealt with this:

> Some people think I'm white, others think I'm more mixed. Some people think I'm Spanish, or Colombian. Or some people just think I'm Italian or European. Some people think I'm bitchy, I think it's because of the eyes. I don't really mind it because at the end of the day I know who I am and I don't need anyone else to tell me who I am cos I know my own identity ... I find it quite funny when people come up with places I have never heard of or places where I think, oh wow, I'd love to be from there.

3. Eight respondents who were second generation or multiple heritage thought that they were incorrectly categorised. In six cases, other people's perceptions were incorrect because the women felt that they were seen as black rather than mixed race, but correct in that the women also identified as black or with black culture. Two respondents who self-identified as mixed race, but identified strongly with black culture, felt that to be accepted as black by black people meant having to deny their mixed heritage. Both respondents said that other people made negative assumptions about them because of their colour, and placed an emphasis on the importance of personality and not colour. Nichole (three quarters Black/a quarter White) drew on the race equals personality correlate in describing how she felt she was seen by others:

> My black identity is very important, but I'd like people to see the person within rather than the person outside, but that's very hard for people to understand at the moment. As soon as people see the colour they think you're this or you're that.

4. Two women felt that they were incorrectly seen as white, and one as 'quarter-caste'. Sherry (Guyanese/German), who thought of herself as dark, and clearly was not white, said that she was seen by others as white. She recalled how as a child she had played mainly with Asian girls, and that everyone had thought she was white. Her comments show how phenotype, or the observable characteristics of a person, and cultural signifiers such as dress and setting contribute to the assump-

tions made about a person. Charmaine (Jamaican/White) was irritated by people's categorisation of her as white:

> When they say I'm white it's not that I don't wanna be white, it's just I wanna be called what I am, there's nothing wrong with being white, but just that I wanna be classed what I am.

Several women talked about being asked the never-ending 'what are you?' question commonly asked of mixed heritage people (Williams, 1996; Parker and Song, 2001, 7). Rosa (Angolan-Portuguese/Portuguese) said:

> Growing up, over the years, I've had a lot of people coming up to me and say 'what are you', and I know what they mean, it's like what's your background, but it's actually made me ask myself what am I? I used to look at my mum and say I'm not the same as her, and I'm not quite as dark as my dad, and I always really felt as if I didn't belong anywhere. I wanted to belong, identify with someone, say I'm the same as that person, which means I'm alright.

Jasmine (Grenadian-Scottish/Dominican) despised this question – *'I'm constantly being asked what are you, what are you, god it's horrible. It makes me feel different and annoyed, it gives me a whole heap of emotions.'* Brenda (Afro-Caribbean/Jewish-Indian) said the question of her race always hung in the air, initially unvoiced but eventually spoken:

> People often like to clarify where I'm from, even though sometimes they don't like to ask – but eventually they will ask, you know, where I am from. That is quite important to them. Until people know what I am they will be a bit more reserved with me. I hope they see more than the colour of my skin. That's quite sad really, isn't it? But you do have some experiences and you do know it's down to the colour of your skin. I thought you were Italian!

Anisha (Indian/white American) felt comfortable with the question, and said:

> I find the more different places I go to, I find the more people ask very early on the 'where are you from' question. They know there's something else about you, so it's trying to figure out the name, trying to figure out the look, something, so I think that's a pretty obvious thing, that people just latch on to whatever they think it is, sometimes guessing what it is.

I was interested to find out whether how the women felt they were seen by others influenced how they saw themselves. Therefore in addition to the question: *How do you think people you don't know see you?* I asked *Does this influence the way you see yourself?* The five pilot study women and five others were not asked this question. The responses were split down the middle: half the women said that how other people saw them did not influence how they saw themselves, and half said that it did.

There was a strong sense of self-affirmation amongst the women who said that how others saw them did not influence their self-perception. The 'I am just me' narrative, also used in the women's definitions of self-hood, was used defiantly in response to the question. Anabel said '*I stand on firm ground*', whilst Sumaira (Pakistani/English) was adamant that '*I do what I want to do, when I want to do it, with who I want to do it, I'm a very stubborn and determined person.*' Kerry, who had been bullied during her school years, said '*When I went to college I was determined just to be me – if people didn't like it then that was tough.*' Peta's comments reveal how self-assertions of being black and white can be linked to the '*I am just me*' narrative:

> I'm white and I'm black, and I do what I want, not what you think I should do. I'm not apologising for who I am. I'm happy about it and if you don't like it – tough.

Corinna (Jamaican/Irish) was rather more nonchalant in her response and said that people's opinions had no affect on her:

> People always say, like, where's your mum from, where's your dad from – I feel no way about it at all. They're trying to put me in a category, but I'm fine to answer their questions. If I was darker they'd see me as black, if I was lighter they'd see me as white ... no matter if I was dark or I was light, I would still see myself as the same.

Feelings of difference

The women were asked the question: *Do you feel different or have you ever felt different to other people?* Over half the sample said that they felt different to others and perceived this difference as negative. Reasons for feeling different included '*looking different*', '*having a foreign accent*', '*race as always being an issue for others*', and '*being treated differently because of colour.*'

Just over one third of the sample either said they had never felt different from other people, or did not have a problem with difference. Chantel (African/English) was ambivalent, and said with an air of inevitability:

> We all feel different, we all feel special, we all feel left out sometimes, we all feel lonely, we all feel popular at different times.

A few of the women who felt different saw difference as a positive thing because they had access to cultures, languages and places which were normally accessible only to white or black people. The celebratory discourse of mixed heritage was clearly evident in the women's talk, and several women suggested that being mixed race was an asset. Olga (Italian/Eritrean), for example, said that she was happy to be mixed because it gave her knowledge about cultures and languages, and made her a more tolerant person. Kerry (English/Bajan) felt she could fit in anywhere:

> I don't think I'd want to be any other race for the pure fact that I can walk into a room and feel comfortable no matter what race there is in the room. I feel I can fit in with people no matter what.

Both Soraya and Jennifer said that they used to experience discrimination, but that they now embraced their difference. Soraya was born in the late 1960s, and Jennifer in the mid 1980s.

> When I was younger I wished I was white so that I wouldn't have any more problems in life, even my name caused problems ... but over time that, if anything, reversed on me. I would get paid compliments for the colour of my skin, compliments for my name because it was unusual, it was different, which made me feel different about myself. Soraya (English/Turkish)

> When I was little I got called racist names about being black, but now I actually get complimented for being mixed race. Now people like it when you've got lots of different cultures in you ... I'm proud of being white, glad I have Irish and black in me. I can find out about different families and things, and it's just nice to have lots of different things in you. Jennifer (Caribbean-Portuguese-Asian/English-Irish)

All the respondents who were either positive or ambivalent about their difference had white fathers and black mothers. Statistically it is far more common for mixed race people to have black fathers and white mothers. More research is needed to find out whether this is significant.

The women were also asked: *Are people curious about your background?* Only a few women responded that people are not especially curious about mixed race people. Chantel said that '*most people don't care about the race thing*', whilst Lianne said '*so many people nowadays are mixed race – if it was a new thing then they would, obviously [be curious].*'

An overwhelming three quarters of the sample said that people were curious about their backgrounds: half of these women said that this was a positive thing, whereas the other half perceived it as negative. A typical response amongst those who saw it as positive was that it was a 'good thing' because it meant that people could '*learn more about different cultures and religions*'. A few women said that this made them feel good about themselves. The number of women who saw curiosity as a positive thing is surprising since only five respondents talked about their own difference as positive, and the majority of women felt that they were wrongly categorised by other people, and this was seen as negative. This apparent discrepancy suggests that the women who saw curiosity as positive may have believed that it could be a way of overcoming mis-categorisation and discrimination. They may have perceived themselves as harbingers of a more egalitarian and culturally aware society, reflecting the public and media discourse which celebrates mixed heritage people as embodiments of diversity and equality.

On discrimination
Daily experiences: '*People judge me because of the colour of my skin*'

The discrimination experienced by mixed heritage people has been recognised as different from the discrimination experienced by people with two black parents or two white parents because they may experience it from both black and white people (Tizard and Phoenix, 2001; DfES, 2004). In her study of mixed race children, Ali (2003) observed that race and racism were not always the most salient issues in the children's lives: they were more concerned with colourism, culturism and nationalism, and race was often conflated with ideas around culture and religion. Given the conflation of race with culture, nationality and religion in the women's talk about what mixed race meant to them, it is possible that they also fused different types of discrimination such as racism and culturism.

This section explores what the women said about their experiences of discrimination. They were asked the question: *Have you ever experienced any discrimination?* I report what the women said but do not analyse what they meant by their replies. The experiences of discrimination the women talked about always related to race, never to gender or class. General experiences of discrimination, and discrimination within the family and from black people were the main issues flagged up in the women's talk. These findings refer specifically to experiences of discrimination in their everyday lives, and not to education, which is discussed later.

Only four women said they had not experienced discrimination. Nine women talked about minor incidents which they described as '*not really*' discrimination. Adriana did not think she had experienced discrimination because being the '*odd one out*' was nothing unusual, and discrimination was inevitable and therefore not really discrimination. Anisha, who had felt acutely aware of her difference as a child and had attempted to reinvent herself as white, said '*I've been teased and made fun of, but I don't think I've been discriminated against.*' Chantel, one of the few women who mentioned gender, remarked that gender discrimination was just as prevalent as racial discrimination.

The majority of women, 27 altogether, explicitly stated that they had experienced discrimination. The experiences ranged widely in both type and quantity. Whilst some women talked about '*little things*' such as name-calling, and things which '*happen all the time*' such as queue jumping, other responses were '*I could go on for hours*' and '*tons, absolutely tons*'. Types of discrimination talked about were bullying at school, rejection, exoticism, institutional racism, and discrimination within the family. How different types of discrimination related to different types of mixed heritages is beyond the scope of this research. Discrimination from white people was referred to dismissively, as if it were irrelevant, whereas discrimination from black people was frequently talked about by the women, and described as overt.

Anita's (Mauritian/Filipino) quote is an example of how discrimination can be subjectively perceived as trivial:

> I've been called Paki a few times by someone in a van, but I didn't really mind cos I knew I'm not from there and they're just racist, they are no one important to me. So it didn't affect me, I started laughing, it just doesn't matter.

Dianne (Welsh/Mauritian) also normalised discrimination, yet beneath the surface a sense of frustration can be detected. Initially she said she had never experienced discrimination, yet within seconds revealed that she had:

> No, not at all, never. Actually my sister looks white although she is half Mauritian. When they see me in Cambridge they look at me as if I'm some sort of alien because down there you won't find any ethnics, and when they do see one they make a judgement of you as if you're a thug or a bad person. It makes me feel horrible because people judge me because of the colour of my skin or race or cultural background, because I think it is wrong to judge people before you actually know them.

Discrimination from black people: 'Not black enough'

In recent years there has been increasing recognition that discrimination can take different forms. Paul Connolly (1998) warned that

> We cannot assume that racism will always be associated with beliefs about racial inferiority; that it will always be signified by skin colour; that it will only be white people who can be racist. (p10)

Gillborn (1996) remarked that whilst black and Asian people can be said to be relatively powerless in the macro context, they can also exercise power and act in a racist manner towards their peers in micro settings such as the school (p170).

Several first generation black/white women talked about being discriminated against by black people. In this kind of discrimination, black people discriminate against mixed race people because of their race or colour, and on account of 'not being black enough', 'acting too white' and/or 'selling out' to the white establishment. The danger, as Clare Gorham (*The Guardian*, 2003) has pointed out, is that 'Black people see degrees of blackness – and in some cases, the wrong shade of black' (p35). Jasmine (Grenadian-Scottish/Dominican) felt discriminated against by black people for not being black enough and, in the context of education, for acting 'too white'.

> It's like, who wants to accept you? They don't want to accept you as being black and they really don't want to accept you as being white, so what am I?

This notion of not being black enough draws on a race essentialist discourse and evokes the idea of racial impurity through blood mixing. It brings to mind the one-drop rule. However, whilst traditionally this rule meant that one drop of black blood made a person black, in this context one drop of white blood made a person white, and was the justification for discrimination and rejection. Tasha said that she experienced racial discrimination and that black men taunted her when they saw her with her white children. This was because black people were '*more into the idea of a black community*'. Cassandra (Jamaican/ Irish) also referred to the idea of the black community. She expressed a sense of resignation, contending that there has been little progress in suturing racial divisions:

> Yeah, like some black people yeah, think like, cos know back in the day used to be like blacks on one side and whites on the other, a lot of racism used to be going on, like I was on the bus and I heard someone say that, ah, mixed race people they shouldn't be made, black people should stay with black people and white people should stay with white people. Like when you listen to [names music band], some black people think that half-caste people shouldn't listen to it, cos they got a part of white inside.

Kim (African [Cuban-Jamaican]/English) also gave her view of black people:

> Black people are often set in their ways, they only listen to particular music, don't want to hear anything new or are only interested in black people who have done something ... white people are often more open to differences between people.

Weekes (1997), drawing on US research, has claimed that acceptable blackness is defined in terms of an essentialist construction of Black womanhood, which is determined by the length and texture of a woman's hair, her skin shade, and frequently her parentage. She has argued that these perceptions come from the idea that black women learn a one dimensional version of blackness within their own community which gives them a sense of relative empowerment (p113). Creating essentialised identities on the basis of skin colour and hair texture, therefore, places many individuals with mixed parentage on the 'boundaries' of blackness (Weekes, 1997).

Three second generation women specifically talked about being on the wrong side of the boundary of blackness. Hair, eye and skin colour were often mentioned by the women generally, and notably in this context. Nalia (three quarters Black/a quarter Chinese) said that she was singled out at school because of her '*reddish hair*', and was often told '*you got something in you.*' Nichole (three quarters Black/a quarter White), who self-defined as mixed race, chose to hide this identity from black people:

> I have black people coming up to me and asking me if I'm mixed race cos I've got green eyes, and I say no I'm not, I deny it. I don't mention that my mother is half-white – I might say it to a mixed race or a white person, but they usually think I'm black anyway.

For some first generation black African or Caribbean/white women especially, assertions of mixed heritage identity meant defying pressures to ally themselves with their black side only. In defining who they were, these women effortlessly juxtaposed their unique individualities with their mixed heritages: '*I am black and I am white, I am just me*'. Lesley (Bajan/Scottish) and Jennifer (Caribbean-Asian-Portuguese/English-Irish) both felt that other people categorised them as black, but that they had to defend their whiteness in situations where they witnessed black people criticising white people. Lesley oscillated between feeling angry about black people denying her mixedness, and normalising discrimination because of its familiarity to her:

> It's mainly young black people talking about white people. They come out with rubbish and say 'no offence' – that really bugs me. I have to defend my whiteness in those situations. Sometimes I have to say like, excuse me, my mum's white you know, and they'll say but I'm not talking about your mum, something stupid like that, they just don't get the point. People like that I can't be bothered to explain myself to.

It becomes too familiar to me, I defend it, and then I forget about it. But I don't want to let them get away with that, what they just said to me.

Jennifer, who asserted '*I am not afraid to say I'm mixed*', said that her whiteness was just as relevant as her blackness:

I've had people try and say to me you're more black because my skin's dark, but I say to them I'm just as much black as I am white because at the end of the day my mum's white and my dad's black so I'm mixed. It doesn't bother me now because everyone seems to know that everyone has got a bit of something different in them.

Danielle (Jamaican/English) talked about feeling in between as a mixed race person. She drew on race essentialist discourse in her talk, and suggested that it was illogical to discriminate against someone who had the same biological or racial make-up. Her black friends perceived her as black and were racist about white people in her presence. White people rejected her because they assumed that she was '*like black people*' and did not realise that she was actually '*like them*':

[On black people] They don't think about half my family being white – because it's part of me, but they don't think of me being different to them.

[On white people] I have always felt with some of the white people I've met that they think I'm not part of their race, they just brush me off and think oh mixed race people are like black people. They don't take in that, I don't like saying this, but that half of me is like them basically.

Similarly, Corinna (Jamaican/Irish) naturalised a race logic which made some people the logical victims of race discrimination, and others such as mixed race people the illogical victims because they had white in them. Therefore, Corinna believed that her biological make-up protected her from racism. She said she had only ever experienced discrimination from her Irish uncle who had pushed her down the stairs when she was six years old because she was black:

That's the only discrimination I've ever had in my life, that was it. I think I've been protected from that cos I'm mixed race. I mean obviously it's not going to stop it, people are always going to be racist and discriminate, but being mixed race I think it does, it shields you because people can't, if they throw abuse at you, if they're white they realise that you've got some white in you.

Kerry (English/Bajan) said that she was bullied at school by a group of black girls because she was '*not black enough*', and went around with a group of white girls. She also talked to white boys, which the black girls did not like. Like several other respondents, Kerry normalised the discrimination she experienced, describing it as '*racism in a way, but more kind of a bitchy power thing, you know, you think you're better than us*'. She drew on race essentialist discourse in which a person's race determined whether they were acceptable or not. In some circumstances it was advantageous to be mixed race and have black and white '*in you*':

> I think that some people are more willing to accept mixed race people than what they are to accept like a white person or a black person. If someone doesn't like black people, sometimes they'll accept a mixed race person cos they've got white in them, but if a black person doesn't like white people they won't accept you cos you got white in you.

Discrimination within the family: '*I almost removed myself from myself*'

One quarter of the sample talked about discrimination within the family: several women talked about their experiences of derision and abuse. Sumaira (Pakistani/English) said that when she was still living at home her stepmother had been abusive, telling her she had '*pig's blood*', amongst other things. Despite this, Sumaira continued to talk to her '*out of respect.*' She found a way of resisting her stepmother's controlling behaviour by living a double life: '*At home I was a quiet obedient little child, when I was out I was wild.*' Latesha (English/Jamaican) and Cassandra (Jamaican/Irish), both 16 years old, said that they were ridiculed for looking different from other family members. Cassandra's black heritage had been kept hidden from her as a child. Latesha said her mother made fun of her colour, but she seemed resigned to this: '*My mum calls me yellow. She's just messin' about but, sometimes that gets on my nerves but, that's just life.*'

Lesley (Bajan/Scottish) said that she learnt the truth about her family as she got older: whereas her white grandparents treated her and her siblings '*no differently*', her black father was treated '*like shit.*' She said her mother had excused her parents' racist behaviour, and justified it by saying that they came from Scotland where there were no black people. Lesley said she hated her grandparents, was furious with her mother, and adamantly defended her father. Her mother no longer had contact with her parents.

Ruby had a Punjabi Indian birth father and an Irish birth mother, and had been adopted by white parents, an Irish mother and an English father. She said that the nuns in the Catholic mother and baby home where she was born had told her birth mother that keeping her baby would be a constant reminder to her of the sin she had committed in being with an Indian man. Ruby's adoptive family had also denied her Indian and Irish heritage. Ruby talked about the legacy of all this, and how she had felt unacceptable because so much to do with her identity was considered unacceptable by others. Through being with other people who had also experienced marginalisation, she could start to accept herself:

> My whole life is predicated on the fact that my parents couldn't, it just wasn't acceptable the relationship that they had, I was not acceptable. It was unacceptable that my birth mother could keep me because I was mixed, and my search for my identity, this experience, is very much woven through this. And equally my upbringing, of being brought up working-class English – there have been a lot of external influences that have determined what was and was not acceptable. So it wasn't acceptable to be Indian, it wasn't acceptable to be Irish, it wasn't acceptable to be working-class – so I almost removed myself from myself.

> The way others see me has had a tremendous impact. It's taken me a long time to learn to trust myself and the way I see myself. It was not only important to deny my Indian but also my Irish background – even my mother denied my Irishness because I was brought up in England, and I was the enemy for her. A few years ago I started meeting people who had been brought up in similar circumstances to my own and that's when I stopped feeling so different, people who had not only had racism outside the home, but also racial prejudice within the home. In trying to be accepted I denied a part of myself, especially my Asian heritage, in my late teens. Then I started to accept myself less as other people saw me, but on positive attitudes rather than seeing myself in negative terms. The change has been more a gradual thing, and in a way it still goes on.

Ruby recalled an incident in childhood when she brought home a tin of curry powder and her mother had screamed at her and left the house, refusing to come back until Ruby had taken the curry powder out of the house. Her explanation for this behaviour was that her mother had herself experienced discrimination as an Irish woman in England in the 1960s. Ruby's experiences of discrimination, and her subsequent removal of herself from herself, was part of the process of bringing her closer to who she felt she really was:

> My search is to be at peace with myself and to be at peace with all these different parts of myself that have caused a great deal of difficulty. It's reclaiming what was denied, it doesn't matter about Irish-ness, Asianness. Regardless of my racial heritage – it's how to feel good about myself.

Most women said that their situation had improved. It seems that, to varying degrees, the women had undergone a process of self-examination in which they re-evaluated their relationships with family members to gain a deeper understanding of the discrimination they had experienced. A sense of loyalty to parents was palpable. Perhaps this loyalty existed, paradoxically, because of the fragile nature of the women's relationships with their families, the constant challenges they faced because they were mixed race, and the possibility of rejection by both sides for not being 'enough' of either side.

The interview data in this chapter support certain findings from earlier studies of mixed race identity such as non-acceptance within peer groups, rejection within families, and ostracism from one or other cultural heritage (see Gibbs, 1997). The ways in which the women's identities were constructed in mono-racial terms by others, and the types of discrimination they experienced, suggest that society is not moving beyond race. This contradicts the popular discourse of heterogeneous identity, in which mixed heritage people are culturally valorised, and race is no longer an important issue. Whilst the increasing number of mixed race people is contributing to the development of an alternative race consciousness which goes beyond normative homogenous constructions of race, race essentialist thinking remains dominant.

5

Evolution and transition

This chapter explores whether, and how, the women felt their perceptions of self had changed over time or due to some turning point in their lives. I expected the shifts in understandings around mixed race, particularly since it has been recognised as an official identity, to be reflected in the data. A powerful link was evident between the women's self-perception and how they felt they were perceived by others. The women talked about their dislike of mono-heritage categorisations, the significance of parental heritage in their constructions of selfhood and their experiences of discrimination.

Personal evolutions: '*Seeing myself through others to seeing myself as myself*'

The question asked was: *Do you feel that your sense of self has changed over time or due to some turning point in your life?* Around three quarters of the sample talked about how their sense of self had changed over time. Many women spoke about their experiences in ways which showed they had given much thought to this question. There was a strong correlation between self and other in these articulations: many women said that negative responses from others prompted negative self-perceptions and that positive responses encouraged positive self-images. Personal transitions involved a shift from '*pleasing others to pleasing myself*' or '*seeing myself through others to seeing myself as myself*'. These changes often involved a transition from identifying with one parental heritage to identifying with both parental heritages. Anabel (Guyanese/Indian-White) described her transition:

Yes, I remember trying to please everybody, so more or less adopting different roles to please everybody. The turning point was about five years ago when I realised how exhausting it had become, mentally and physically, that's when I began the journey towards personal wholeness, my identity as a person in my own right where I was pleasing myself and not the whole world as such.

The women's personal evolutions generally corresponded with having greater contact with mixed heritage people and living in a diversely populated place such as London. The greater the exposure to difference the less the respondent saw her own difference as negative. Younger respondents frequently commented on the prevalence of mixed race people and the normality of being mixed race in multicultural areas of London today. Personal evolution was talked about by older respondents and by 16 and 17 year-olds. Jennifer (Caribbean-Asian-Portuguese/English-Irish), who was 17, said that when she was at school she was accepted because she

> ... acted in a certain way, the way they liked it ... but now I've grown up a bit more I feel I'm not white, I'm not black, I'm mixed, I am who I am, I just feel I'm not trying to copy anyone now. It was when I started to hang out with mixed race girls that I started to feel more free to act as I want.

Diverse environments and the increased visibility of mixed heritage people, whilst experienced as positive by some women because it allowed them to assert their mixed heritage identity, also made some women feel more self-conscious about their difference. Cassandra (Jamaican/Irish), who was 16, had spent part of her childhood in Spain before moving to London. She grew up with her white mother, white step-father, and white siblings, and had only been told as a teenager that her real father was black. For Cassandra, problems relating to her identity began when she learnt that she was mixed race.

> When I was younger I used to think that I was brought up in Spain and that I had a tan, cos I never knew that my dad was black. I thought my sister's dad and my brother's dad was mine. We don't look nothing alike, like when I say that's my sister, they say, no, it's not.

Tasha (black American/English), who had grown up and until recently lived in Cambridge, had always classed herself as black '*cos I grew up in a place predominantly white and the way other people saw me made me feel more black.'* Tasha now described herself as mixed race because that was how black people saw her. She said she had never felt different until she moved to London:

> In a multicultural place like London you are always asked what you are, whereas in Cambridge, if you're a slightly different colour, you are just classed as black.

Tasha did not feel different being black in a mainly white environment, but did feel different being mixed race in a racially mixed area of London. Tasha's explanation for this was that in London *'cultures tend to stick together'*, and that even mothers who took their kids to school were *'segregated.'*

Denial, invention and retrieval

This section focuses on what four women, Frida (Colombian/Polish Jewish-English), Anisha (Indian/white American), Kim (African [Cuban-Jamaican]/English) and Rosa (Angolan-Portuguese/Portuguese), said about their experiences of identity transition. They talked about their paths to self-acceptance, and their journeys encompass the range of experiences which have already been discussed: mis-categorisation, feelings of difference and non-acceptance, and being discriminated against. Ruby's talk in the section on discrimination in the last chapter showed the overlap between the profound influence other people had on her, her experiences of discrimination within the family, and her subsequent denial of her Indian and Irish heritage. These themes are further explored here.

The women all talked about reclaiming the part or half of their identity which had previously been denied or lain dormant: this was always the minority parental heritage, and in all cases the father's heritage. The process of transition was described by the women as a shift towards identifying with both parental heritages and seeing and accepting themselves as mixed race. All the women said that being wrongly categorised had influenced the way they saw themselves, and that the ensuing feeling of difference was why they tried to reclaim the part that was missing. They all sought to retrieve the missing part of themselves to create a sense of wholeness, a sense of who they really were.

Frida grew up with her Polish Jewish-English mother and had a Jewish upbringing. She did not know her Colombian father, and described the lack of knowledge about this side of her heritage as a gap, and as something that was denied her. In her late teens, Frida became increasingly interested in her Colombian heritage, and filled the gap in her life by inventing herself as Colombian. She learned Spanish and began to have more contact with Latin American people, then married a Colombian and had a child with him.

As a child people thought she was Pakistani, and Frida believed that being wrongly categorised contributed to her inventing herself as Latin American. She experienced what might be called a double denial: first her Colombian heritage was denied and her identity was also denied by those who wrongly categorised her as Asian. Frida's indignation about being mis-categorised was less to do with discriminating against Asian people than with her desire to be seen for who she really was. Her talk shows how the various themes – mis-categorisation, the denial of her true heritage, discrimination, drawing on both parental heritages in the assertion of her identity, and asserting selfhood against others – are connected in her invention of herself:

> I became much more aware of a Latin, I don't know, something Latin about me, almost like I could put a label on myself sometimes like I'm not Asian, I don't know, it's difficult to explain. In one sense I don't like being categorised or categorising, but there was this phase of me reinventing myself or adding to myself, and that is me purposefully consciously saying I want to make this part of me. I remember as a child they used to take the mickey out of me and call me Paki or whatever, and I'd be like 'look, if you're gonna be racist then just get it right, don't ass ... you know, call me what I am!' I don't know, I don't like it, I don't like being put into that, I think cos I feel like I'm not that and I don't relate to that ... in one sense it's negative cos I'm putting Asian into a category, but just from my experience of Asian people, I don't want to be categorised like that. On the other hand I don't mind people categorising me as Latin cos I quite like to have that identity to a degree, maybe cos I felt like I didn't have it as a child, and it's almost like in my adulthood I've recreated a part of myself and had links with a whole other world which I didn't really know much about.

Anisha, who grew up with both her parents in a white environment in the States, said that she felt extremely unattractive as a child – '*I was told by a boy I went to school with that I look like a monkey.*' As a result she was introverted and '*very into her library books*'. Constant questions about her identity from her Indian relatives and children at school made her feel insecure about her identity and gave her a negative image of her Indian heritage.

> My father's relatives came to stay when I was young and there were always questions about my name and why I looked different, and religion-wise too – all my friends were Christian and went to church and Sunday school and I didn't know anything about that. Being half Indian I was different and people couldn't figure out what it was, they thought I must be Italian, that's as exotic as they could think. I was embarrassed about my father, I thought people would look at him and not understand where he came from and that he spoke funny English.

Anisha talked about two main turning points in her life. The first, at the age of 9, involved the denial of the Indian side of her heritage, which was effectively a denial of her father, and the invention of herself as white. She realised that she could fight back against being constructed as Indian by simply refusing everything Indian:

> It had built up and at that age I realised that I could actually do things that could enable me to reject it, I didn't just have to be upset about those things, but I could say well I've got a second name I can use, I don't have to eat this food, I can tell people my father is the neighbour, I can make up stories, I don't have to be this person. I went by my middle name which is Christine, because Anisha was too foreign, because I didn't want people to know who my father was, I didn't want to have anything to do with anything that was Indian.

The second turning point for Anisha came at the age of 14 or 15, when she was '*getting over puberty and a physically awkward period*', and meeting new people outside school. This involved the retrieval of her Indian heritage, and an affirmation of her mixed heritage. She started to use the name Anisha again. Despite the questions and taunts from others as a child and a teenager, she believed she must have been getting some positive signals about her difference and the way she looked, and this helped her to see that being part-Indian was *'alright, and even a good thing'*:

> I began to feel comfortable about how I looked, and then I realised that the way I looked had to do with where my parents come from, and maybe it's an advantage to look a bit different, not to look like every blond blue-eyed person around you. I think when I had the reverse, you know, kind of accepting again, that was more subtle. I think that happened over time.

Kim talked about two turning points as a teenager. First, she used her mixed heritage to make herself acceptable to others, especially men. The celebration discourse of mixed race is evident in Kim's quote, and like so many advertisements which contain images of mixed heritage women, is heavily gendered in tone:

> At 13 I looked like a boy, boys took no interest, they only liked blond blue-eyed girls. Then I grew my hair and older men liked me, I was always told what a nice mix I am, that Jamaican/English was the best mix, got loads of positive feedback from what I looked like. So I went from ugly duckling to what everyone wants and my head got enormous. By 15 I was the best I'd ever looked, but I also realised the only reason men were interested was because of the way I looked – because I was mixed, not black or white.

Like Anisha, Kim's second turning point came at around the age of 15. She realised she wanted to be seen *'as me, as a person who is Kim is Kim, that has nothing to do with the actual race'*, and stopped exoticising herself. Kim talked about gaining a stronger sense of herself in this process of transition, in which she reversed the self/other logic: *'Now how I see myself will be how you see me. If I wait for you to make a judgement about how I am, and behave the way you expect me to, then I'm not being myself.'*

Rosa's mother was white Portuguese and her father mixed race Portuguese-Angolan, and she grew up with both parents in a mainly white family and environment. Rosa, like Anisha and Kim, also talked about her identity transition as manifesting itself in two stages. The first stage, like Frida, involved the invention of the dormant minority heritage, and the second turning point involved a shift from identifying mainly with her black heritage to *'accepting herself as herself'*.

Rosa's first turning point came at the age of 15, when she began to realise that her feeling of being black overrode any insistence by her parents that she was white. Rosa talked about two main experiences which contributed towards her *'leaning towards black'*. She experienced racial discrimination at the convent school she attended until she was 16, where the white girls would scrub her hands with a nailbrush *'cos they were trying to get my skin white'*; and her parents categorically denied her mixed heritage. Rosa's father's refusal to acknowledge his own black heritage ultimately led her to valorise her own black heritage. Being black took on exaggerated meaning for Rosa in that she lived her father's heritage for him. For Rosa, being black was about feeling black, regardless of skin colour.

> My dad has lots of issues with being black – he is black, but will die before telling you he is black. He's Portuguese and refuses to accept blackness. Black men, he says, are good for two things – breeding women, leaving them, and drugs. They said black is no good, they tried to brainwash me into believing I am white and that white is better than being black. I was desperately looking to him for support, for him saying it was alright to be black, but my dad didn't see it. Maybe that pushed me towards the black culture more, because they were so desperately trying to deny its existence.

> It's how I feel inside because my parents would say you're Portuguese, but I don't feel in the least bit Portuguese – so I think it comes from within, it's how I feel within – which is black. I don't think how black you are has got anything to do with your skin at all. It's what goes on in here [points to her head] and in here [points to her heart].

Rosa's second turning point occurred in the last few years, and involved the transition from identifying solely with her black heritage to seeing herself as a person in her own right. When people come up to her these days and say 'what are you?' her response is *'first of all I'm a person before anything else'*. Rosa said that she now possessed a strength which enabled her to recognise how her past experiences had contributed to who she was today. Her tone was defiant:

> When I was younger I did have a hell of a lot of issues around colour. I think mainly what its stem was, was the need to belong and not knowing well am I black am I white am I Portuguese am I English am I that am I

this, there were so many questions in my mind and my parents didn't help me at all, so they probably added to my confusion. I've only come to the conclusion that I am me regardless of my colour in the last two or three years. Now I'm strong enough to say I'm me, sod you lot – even though I identify more with the black culture, the bottom line is I don't give a toss about anyone else, this is me, you can either like it or lump it.

All the women invented themselves in different ways. Whilst Anisha denied her mixed heritage and presented herself as white, and Kim accentuated her mixed heritage, the intention was similar: both women sought to define themselves in ways which would make them more acceptable to other people. Frida and Rosa invented themselves in the bid to reclaim their denied heritages. Both of them displayed what Ifek-wunigwe (1999) has referred to as a 'hyper black' identity, an opposi-tional identity which mixed heritage people seek out when undergoing some challenge which forces them to question their predominantly white identities. In all four cases the women's second turning points in-volved resisting the roles or identities which had in some way been determined by others. Anisha rejected her father's Indian heritage and later reclaimed it, Kim deliberately over-stated her mixed heritage to be acceptable and then accepted herself as herself, Frida and Rosa both felt that access to their fathers' cultural heritage had been denied, and actively invented these heritages and incorporated them into their own lives and identities. For these women, the quest for a sense of whole-ness was the driving force behind the denial and invention of identity.

Identity: concluding remarks

This section draws together the findings of the previous three chapters on the women's everyday experiences of identity. The themes of race and heritage were expressed in the women's talk about how they de-fined themselves, their friendships, how they were perceived by others, feelings of difference, adapting in different situations, experiences of discrimination, and how they felt their identities had changed over time. A complex picture of mixed heritage identity emerges: the dis-courses of essentialism, postmodernism and individualism were drawn upon in their talk, and these discourses were both overlapping and contradictory.

Essentialist discourse was reproduced in the women's assertions of both sides of their heritage, and in the way they constructed their identity in opposition to homogeneous categories of identity. Identities and allegiances were sometimes constructed in opposition to black people: one could argue that these constructions were defensive positions, arising out of mis-categorisation and discrimination. The findings suggest that there was a link between other people's denial and the women's assertion of mixed heritage identity. Postmodernist discourse was drawn upon in the women's general definitions of mixed heritage, in their diverse concepts of friendship, and how they defined their identity as changing over time: as heterogeneous, shifting, denied and invented. The individualist discourse was drawn upon in that many women saw themselves as unique mixed heritage individuals and constructed personhood in autonomous terms in which race did not impact on people's lives or core personalities.

The emphasis on race in the women's talk confounds the postmodernist notion that race can be transcended and that people are inherently free to choose their identities. At the same time, the women's assertions of their individuality and the rejection of race as a concept, suggests that they were comfortable with the idea of going beyond race.

Given that most of the women were probably from working-class backgrounds, this raises the question of whether the postmodern discourse of mixed heritage is a middle-class discourse, one which speaks mainly though mixed heritage people who are privileged and/or identify with middle-class values, and whether essentialist discourse is drawn upon more readily by people who feel marginalised and discriminated against. Recent research by Caballero (2007) has shown that only middle class parents in their study viewed their children's identities as 'open' in a cosmopolitan sense, whereas identities were expressed as 'open', 'mixed' or 'single' by parents across all classes.

A discussion of the interplay between mixed heritage, class and popular discourses is beyond the reach of this book; the findings, however, show that it is imperative to continue research which investigates how mixed heritage identity is shaped by class and gender, and constructed in a variety of ways through language and discourse.

Chantel's (English/African) quote indicates how attitudes around race may be shifting. Only a few years ago one of Ifekwunigwe's (1999) project participants said: '*Eventually, that moment comes when we look in the mirror and we see what a bi-razialised society tells us we must see – a Black woman ...*' For Chantel, however, looking in the mirror was about understanding herself in ways which had nothing to do with race.

> I sometimes hear people say 'I look in the mirror and I know it's a black person standing there, know it's a white person standing there, know it's a half-caste person standing'. I look in the mirror and I think 'I know it's a person standing here who hasn't achieved everything they need to, who needs to go out today' ... I don't think about the colour of my skin, I just never think about them kind of things, not because I never have, I just don't think it's important.

The next three chapters look at education. Education is a significant aspect of identity, and the purpose of these chapters is to focus on how the women positioned themselves in relation to prevailing government and policy discourses around education. The women's constructions of identity show how the discourses of essentialism, postmodernism and individualism interplayed. The policy and interview data on education show that the discourse of individualism was dominant.

6

Investigating education policy

C hapter Six discusses wider government discourses around education, and analyses discourses on equity and personhood identified in a selection of post-compulsory education policy documents published in Britain since 1997. It provides the discursive framework for the women's reflections on their experiences of education and education policy discourses, which are explored in Chapter Seven.

This chapter opens with a brief background to the concept of the liberal individual, and how this concept is used in contemporary discourse. The main post-1997 discourses of economic efficiency and social justice are then examined, in which lifelong learning for economic and personal development, social inclusion, equality of opportunity and individual responsibility are dominant themes. The FE context is also considered.

The second part of the chapter examines three post-compulsory education policy documents published since 1997 for their discourses around equity and personhood. The three documents are *Learning for the Twenty-first Century* (Fryer, 1997), *The Learning Age: A Renaissance for a new Britain* (Green Paper) (DfEE, 1998) and *Learning to Succeed: A new framework for post-16 learning* (White Paper) (DfEE, 1999). A green paper is published by the government on a specific policy area, and is usually addressed to interested parties who are invited to participate in a process of consultation and debate, which may form the basis for subsequent legislation. A white paper may follow a green paper, and contains official proposals and recommendations for specific policy areas. Ozga's model (outlined in Chapter One) is used. The documents are examined for the stories they present around equity and person-hood, how people are represented within the framework of inclusion and exclusion, and how the policies construct subjecthood (Ozga, 2000).

The wider context: concepts and discourses
Liberalism and the concept of the individual

There are two types of liberalism: political and economic. Both are committed to an ideology of individualism in which the individual is a socially and culturally decontextualised self, a coherent unitary ego capable of rational choice. Political liberalism focuses on Kant's concept of autonomy and the imperative of formal rights (Reiss, 1991). It assumes the freedom of the individual and her or his ability to act and make choices independently. Economic liberalism views people as rational utility maximisers. This type of liberalism is based on the poli-tical obligation of the individual to the state in a possessive market society, where everyone is subject to the market and sees the inherent 'rightness' of political authority (MacPherson, 1962). The rights of the individual are therefore framed within a contract between the indivi-dual and the state, and can be understood as the normative expecta-tions which specify the relationship between the state and its individual members.

The concept of liberalism has shifted historically in relation to dominant discourses prevalent in political and economic fields at dif-ferent times. The type of liberalism we have today in Britain is new liberalism, or neo-liberalism. The focus of the state is not on the indivi-dual as an autonomous rational being, as in political liberalism, but on his or her role in the global marketplace. Self-interest and the interests of the government are therefore seen as synonymous in that both the individual and the state are unequivocal beneficiaries. Critics of this view have argued that people are simply understood as self-interested utility maximisers who turn themselves into market individuals (Peters, 1996). This new economic discourse may be understood as a new meta-narrative which justifies all forms of economic development.

One strand of recent social theory has focused on the processes and pressures of individualisation within the neo-liberal discourse. Gordon (1991) has argued that neo-liberalism institutionalises enterprise as a general organising principle for society – a 'global re-description of the social as a form of the economic' – in which the individual becomes the entrepreneur of her or himself (p44). Similarly, Rose (1992) has pointed out that liberal governments have always been concerned with in-culcating their authority on citizens through developing and enhancing programmes and techniques that will simultaneously 'autonomize' and 'responsibilize' subjects (p162). Thus, in the current climate of new liberalism, the emphasis is on the right and capability of the individual to secure a future of her or his own choosing, and the discourse of com-petitiveness in which each individual is supposed to serve a function based on the logic of capitalism. In the next section the dominant UK government discourses around education are examined.

Economic competitiveness and social justice

Western democracies such as Britain have been faced with the problem of how best to reconcile an inclusive society based on egalitarian prin-ciples and a learner-centred approach which stresses individual rights, with capital accumulation and economic efficiency (Whitty *et al*, 1997). This dilemma has arisen out of the perceived need to keep pace with globalisation, and the recognition that alienating those at the bottom end of the market is not the way forward for global competition (Brown and Lauder, 2000). Equality and how to ensure that disadvantaged people are not excluded from basic rights through market-driven mechanisms has become one of the primary goals in public sector areas such as health and education (Ozga, 2000).

The ideological context in which New Labour's education policies were to be established was already developed by the mid 1990s. The em-phasis on post-compulsory education and training was central to a vision of a competitive and just society in which education not only contributed to a high value-added economy, but also played a role in solving the problem of unemployment. Education and training would lead Britain to be transformed from a low-skill, low-wage economy to a high-skill, high-wage technological economy (Tomlinson, 2001). The government made education its main priority, signified by the now well-known mantra 'education, education, education'. Following this shift in focus from markets *per se* to lifelong learning, the two dominant discourses in education since 1997 have been economic efficiency and social justice. The related discourses of the value of education, learning for economic and personal reward, equality of opportunity, merito-cracy, social inclusion and individual responsibility are implicit within these discourses.

Lifelong learning has been described by the European Commission (2001) as all learning which aims to 'improv[e] knowledge, skills and competences, within a personal, civic, social and/or employment-related perspective' (p9). Lifelong learning as a major theme within post-16 education and training policies underpinned the government's view that a learning society should be promoted on the principles of individual responsibility, investment in people, and a progressive learn-ing market (Tomlinson, 2001). The belief that British society was class-less, and that individual effort and merit would result in educational, occupational and social mobility was related to this view. The chairman of the National Campaign for Learning explained his vision of a Learn-ing Society for the UK: '... the key principle governing provision for and pursuit of learning in the future must be the primacy of personal res-ponsibility for learning ... The focus of the campaign will be on indivi-duals rather than on the providers of education and training' (Ball, 1996 cited in Fryer, 1997).

Some critiques of policy

Critics of current government philosophy and policy have argued that greater emphasis on individual responsibility is one effect of the shift in focus from a concern with equality *per se* to equality of opportunity and social inclusion (Lister, 2001; Colley and Hodkinson, 2001). Although lifelong learning and self-responsibility should in many ways be seen as positive, individual responsibility also means that the government need not acknowledge trenchant structural inequalities (Lister, 2001). Lister claims:

> The goal remains the more limited one of raising the social floor and promoting equality of opportunity rather than addressing wider in-equalities ... On the one hand the privileged can continue to buy their children a preferential start in the meritocratic race; on the other hand

the poverty of those who fail to succeed, despite the opportunities
opened up, is likely to be legitimated by a culture of meritocracy. (p438)

Thus, inequalities in society may be seen as the personal troubles of
individuals without education and skills.

Disadvantage, as Rose (1992) has pointed out, may in fact be understood as deficit or disease which is located within the individual. Colley
and Hodkinson (2001), in their analysis of the Social Exclusion Unit's
report *Bridging the Gap* (1999), have argued that this report 'locates the
causes of social exclusion in the deficits of individuals, and aggregates
those individuals as generalised, and pathologised, social groupings'
(p342). As such, the authors argue, policy is predisposed towards the
idea of non-participants as responsible for changing their own behaviour, in which economic and social exclusion become the inevitable
consequences of non-participation.

There is growing concern that the preoccupation with the market principle, competitiveness and the culture of self-interest is increasingly
geared towards feeding the demands of an enterprise culture, and has
confused the social and moral purposes of education (Ball, 1994, 144).
As Ball has argued: 'The majesty of the market is so stridently
trumpeted by its advocates that all else is in danger of being drowned
out' (p144). It is significant that the market appears to give greater autonomy whilst in fact reinforcing inequalities and advantaging some
people over others, reproducing a division of labour along class lines. In
the 1990s inequalities rose in Britain faster than in any other western
state (Hutton, 1995). Despite the rhetoric of inclusion and meritocracy,
market competition benefits the middle-class and aspiring groups, and
perpetuates a divided and divisive education system (Tomlinson, 2001).

Recent research has shown that whilst people from ethnic minorities
accounted for 13 per cent of students in Higher Education, compared
with 9 per cent of the total population, people from all minority groups
were more likely to be studying at new universities (*Social Trends* 30,
2000: 56 cited in Tomlinson, 2001, 147).

Our supposedly meritocratic system favours those who have already
had an educational head start, and increasingly places an emphasis on
a person's wealth and capacity to buy an education from a reputable

institution, as opposed to their motivations or abilities. Black people, who have a proportionally lower socio-economic standing than white people, are more likely to follow a vocational path, and enter government training and work experience programmes in disproportionate numbers (Mizen, 2003, 471). Certainly, the differences in the student populations in terms of their race and class backgrounds within the elite and new universities in London are striking. The higher achievements of those from higher socio-economic groups and the ensuing rewards are rationalised and validated by the myth of meritocracy. Moreover, it has been shown that class mobility and status determined by merit are limited, and that people from lower socio-economic backgrounds have to demonstrate greater merit to enter desirable class positions (Goldthorpe, 1997).

Universalistic education initiatives and policy formulations which promote equality of opportunity and social inclusion have not affected the continued segregated take-up of education along class and ethnic lines. Perhaps, as Avis *et al* (1996) have argued, the dictum of equality is fundamentally unrealistic because the social inclusion discourse functions within a hegemonic capitalist discourse of competitiveness.

The FE context

Since 1997, the lifelong learning agenda has underpinned programmes of educational reform which aim to support marginalised people and encourage them to take part in education to enhance their chances of success in the labour market. These programmes encompass strategies designed to bring about widened opportunities and increased participation in post-16 education (Keep and Mayhew, 1998, 2000), especially for some ethnic minority groups, adults in unskilled occupations, and people with a background of failure in their schooling (Zera and Jupp, 2000). FE colleges have been seminal in implementing such strategies of inclusion (Kennedy, 1997).

Some educationalists have pointed out that the expansion of participation in post-compulsory education has coincided with the deregulation of education systems in favour of market-led principles. They claim that the quest to redress socio-economic inequalities through social inclusion initiatives, paradoxically, recedes under the new economic discourse of competitiveness (Peters, 1996; Maguire *et al*, 1999). Institutions are expected to function according to a competitive market logic within a state system which utilises national performance criteria, and distributes funding according to the merit and status of institutions, and on a *per capita* basis. This has created a financial relationship between user and provider and competition for potential students, and the survival of educational establishments therefore depends largely on their ability to attract enough and the right kind of students (Burchell, 1993).

Maguire *et al* (1999) have argued that the way in which FE colleges are now funded has generated increased competition, resulting in marketing and promotional expenditure by many college providers which aims to ensure an across the board appeal from pre-vocational through to A-levels. This type of marketing contributes to the reproduction of social differentiation within post-16 education and the racing and classing of institutions.

In terms of gender differentiation, disproportionately more young women than men are educated post-16 in colleges than in schools. In terms of ethnic differentiation, Sixth Form and FE colleges provide for 57 per cent of black 16 year-olds, whilst schools only provide for 22 per cent; moreover, the children of less well educated parents are more likely to be in FE colleges as opposed to schools or higher education (Brown *et al*, 2004). This supports the prevalent view that FE colleges have a lower status than universities.

The FE sector is still the most genuinely inclusive education sector. In the last decade, it has seen the expansion of provision for 16 to 19 year olds, vocational education and training (VET), as well as adult and higher education. FE colleges are the largest providers of VET, and they also offer more academic A-levels than secondary schools. There has been an unprecedented increase in student numbers, and in the academic year 2002/2003 there were more than three times as many full-time and part-time students in FE colleges as in universities (Brown *et al*, 2004). Seventy per cent of 16 year olds (with fewer than five GCSEs at grade A* – C) are in FE colleges (Brown *et al*, 2004), whilst their higher achieving counterparts are in sixth forms and sixth form colleges, and 80 per cent of the FE student cohort are adults over 19 years of age. Research has shown that young people often view FE college as a better option than being in low paid work or at school, and that being treated as an adult is an important reason for studying in further education (Hyland and Merrill, 2003, 90-92).

The next section explores the ways in which the government discourses around national economic competitiveness and social justice, and the related discourses of the value of education, individual responsibility and equality of opportunity, are reflected in the policy documents which have been selected for analysis.

Policy findings
Background to the selected policy documents

The Kennedy Report (June 1997) was the first in a series of reports providing recommendations for further education in the UK. It was set up to consider widening participation in further education and emphasised the importance of post-16 education in creating a 'self-perpetuating learning society' (Kennedy, 1997, 25). This report was followed in September by a report of the National Advisory Group for Continuing Education and Lifelong Learning (NAGfCELL), set up by the Labour government in 1997 and chaired by Bob Fryer, entitled *Learning for the Twenty-First Century* (Fryer, 1997). One main concern was that in comparison to France, Germany, Singapore and the US, countries identified as 'world class standard' (DfEE, 1998, 34), one third of the British population had had no formal education or training since leaving school (Fryer, 1997) and 40 per cent of 18 year-olds were not in any kind of education or training (National Advisory Council for Education and Training Targets [NACETT] cited in Fryer, 1997, 2).

The key aim of Fryer's Report was to make the case for the development of a culture of lifelong learning and achieve a 'Learning Age' in Britain. *Learning for the Twenty-first Century* (Fryer, 1997) was an advisory report for the Green Paper *The Learning Age* (DfEE, 1998), which built on this and focused largely on future policy strategies for lifelong learning and education.

Learning for the Twenty-first Century and *The Learning Age* are both concerned with revealing the extent of the problems of inequity and disadvantage in British society and are idealistic in tone. The policy published subsequently, *Learning to Succeed* (DfEE, 1999), is primarily concerned with pushing for reform. Its aim is to drive up standards and qualifications, and emphasise the link between qualifications, the workplace and the broader economy. The various discursive preoccupations around equity and personhood identified in these policy documents are now explored.

The Labour Government placed economic competitiveness and social inclusion at the centre of education policy goals. The policy documents support these discourses by focusing on economic competitiveness, social inclusion and personal development as the core organising principles around which lifelong learning should be built. The main assumption is that education and learning give the dual benefits of greater potential for economic competitiveness and for making people happy and self-fulfilled (Shackleton 1992, Murphy, 1993, Keep and Mayhew, 1998, 2000 for critiques). The key discourses identified on the policy texts are now discussed.

Learning as an investment for reward

The discourse of learning as an investment for reward is dominant in all the policy documents. It is underpinned by the wider government discourses of economic competitiveness, social inclusion, and the related discourses of the value of education, individual responsibility and equality of opportunity through lifelong learning.

The main idea behind this discourse is that learning extends outwards from the individual to the nation, and spans all of life. In the words of the then Prime Minister, 'education is the best economic policy we have' (DfEE, 1998, 9). The nation and the individual are represented as being the beneficiaries and ultimate winners of investment in learning. The nation benefits because a skilled and educated nation makes Britain a viable economic competitor in the global market. Individuals benefit because greater personal economic prosperity and a higher level of personal and spiritual development can be expected, allowing them to achieve their potential and reap the personal rewards of sovereignty, self-empowerment and success (DfEE, 1999, 6). The function of education is built around the liberal assumption that it can make up for all the deficits in society. The neo-liberal idea that the interests of the nation state and the individual are conflated is embedded within this discourse:

Learning is the key to prosperity – for each of us as individuals, as well as for the nation as a whole. Investment in human capital will be the foundation of success in the knowledge-based global economy of the twenty-first century. This is why the government has put learning at the heart of its ambition.

[On learning] It makes ours a civilised society, develops the spiritual side of our lives and promotes active citizenship. Learning enables people to play a full part in their community. It strengthens the family, the neighbourhood and consequently the nation. (Foreword by David Blunkett, DfEE, 1998, 7)

The principles of lifelong learning provide a rationale for extending learning opportunities throughout the lifespan and to a wide range of participants. The emphasis in the policies is on nurturing the 'intellectual capital' of the nation (DfEE, 1998, 10) and putting 'people before structures' (Fryer, 1997, 29). Personal investment in learning is about developing one's own potential as a social citizen in both economic and personal development terms, and cultivating the skills, knowledge and understanding that are essential for employability and fulfilment. The link between education and personal development draws on the liberal idea of the incomplete self, in which the individual is continuously in the process of realising his or her self-potential. The following quotes express this idea:

Learning is what people do when they want to make sense of experience. It may involve an increase in skills, knowledge, understanding, values, and the capacity to reflect. Effective learning leads to change, development and a desire to learn more (Campaign for Learning cited in Fryer, 1997, 16).

The development of a culture of learning will help to build a united society, assist in the creation of personal independence, and encourage our creativity and innovation. Learning builds self-confidence and independence ... Learning offers excitement and the opportunity for discovery. It stimulates enquiring minds and nourishes our souls. It takes us in directions we never expected, sometimes changing our lives. (DfEE, 1998, 10)

Lifelong learning should be for all aspects of life and meet a variety of needs and objectives. It should foster personal and collective development ... contribute to the enlargement of knowledge itself, enhance cultural and leisure pursuits and underpin citizenship and independent living. (Fryer, 1997, 29)

The key to the success of the nation and the individual ultimately lies in the take up of educational opportunities on offer and personal responsibility for learning. The difficulty is that in putting 'people before structures' the government is effectively denying its own responsibility in addressing educational, social, economic inequalities. In the next section, the dominant discourse of self-responsibility for learning is discussed.

The responsibility of the individual to learn

The policy documents express the idea that the onus of responsibility is on the individual to learn. This discourse of personal responsibility for learning is supported by the wider government discourse of individual responsibility. It is linked to the government's concern with promoting a balance between individuals' rights and responsibilities: in so far as the government makes opportunities available, individuals have a responsibility to take them up. The policies acknowledge that structural mechanisms disadvantage some groups of people, and concede that barriers to access and participation have to be eliminated before equality of opportunity can be achieved. Once the government and education providers have removed all obstacles, however, learning can be effortlessly instilled into the population.

> In setting the new framework, we look to individuals to take responsibility for their own future assisted by intensive advice and support, to seek opportunities to improve their knowledge, understanding and skills; and to make their own investment in personal success. (DfEE, 1999, 15)

The assumption is that a level playing field in terms of access and opportunities is possible, and that internalised personal barriers to learning do not impact on the kinds of choices people make or feel are available to them (Reay *et al*, 2001). The individual is portrayed as a sovereign entity capable of making rational unfettered choices, and able to reap the rewards of learning unencumbered. This issue is discussed more fully in Chapter Seven in relation to the women's attitudes towards and experiences of education.

Personal responsibility for learning is extended to the notion that education is an imperative. In this sense it is actually an 'enforced choice'. This is expressed through the idea that people will be at the mercy of the market economy if they do not continuously upgrade skills. The individual has to recognise that a job for life is a thing of the past (Fryer, 1997, 5) and that 'familiar certainties and old ways of doing things are disappearing' (DfEE, 1998, 9). The Fryer Report (1997) states:

> If people are not to be locked into particular jobs with limited life-chances, risking being marooned by change or denied scope for improvement, they need the generic, core and transferable skills which will strengthen their position in the marketplace. The aim should be to make people less vulnerable, at the same time as enhancing the capacities and competitiveness of businesses and other organisations. (p12)

The emphasis on the idea that the individual has the power to make autonomous choices overlooks the fundamental role the state has in defining the parameters of learning, which confine those choices within the discourse of national economic competitiveness. This is the inherent contradiction between the discourse of the economy and the discourse of the individual. People are purportedly free to make choices, but are compelled to make quite specific choices within the economic framework set out by government. Those who do not take up the opportunities on offer, or make choices which are outside the government framework, are left behind. Ultimately, the wrong choices, failure to participate, ignorance of the opportunities available, and low aspirations all fall back on the individual, and people themselves are deemed responsible for their own exclusion (Tight, 1998a).

Inequity in society

The policy discourse of inequity in society reproduces the wider government discourse of social justice/inclusion. The policy documents acknowledge that there are widening social and economic inequalities, many of which are 'multiple and mutually reinforcing, amounting to compound forms of exclusion on the one hand, and the emergence of a virtual super class of privilege on the other' (Fryer, 1997, 14). The claim is that there is too much focus on successful learners, and too little support for those who lack confidence or believe that education is not for them.

Leaving school early, poverty, lack of qualifications and skills, lack of self-esteem, low status and powerlessness are given as the main factors affecting adult participation in education (Fryer, 1997, 16). One study showed that whilst 80 per cent of 18 year-olds from senior managerial and professional backgrounds went into higher education, only 10 per cent from unskilled backgrounds did so (Dearing cited in Fryer, 1997, 15). Another study claimed that people with poor literacy and numeracy skills were not only at a higher risk of unemployment and having a lower earning capacity, but were also more likely to be in 'poor health or suffer from depression and take less part in community groups and voting in elections' (Basic Skills Agency cited in Fryer, 1997, 15).

Fryer's (1997) report warns of the 'noticeable and dangerous 'learning divide" in which those who are well-qualified tend to continue to be learners throughout life, and those who leave education with few qualifications, or who do not engage in learning as adults, continue to believe that education is not for them (p15). The main prerequisite for the success of a lifelong learning strategy is the development of a positive attitude to learning. Because negative attitudes to learning are so deeply entrenched, a 'culture of learning' should be instilled into those people not engaged in learning. This requires a 'quiet and sustained revolution in aspiration and achievement' (DfEE, 1998, 13). As Fryer has argued:

> The biggest change of all will be required in the attitudes of individuals and groups, particularly amongst those who are not currently engaged in lifelong learning activities, who demonstrate no inclination to become involved, or enjoy few opportunities to develop their abilities, interests or capacities through learning. (p4)

A discourse of the dangers of the 'uneducated individual' can also be identified. This sits alongside the discourse of individual responsibility to produce the idea that those who do not learn will be responsible for perpetuating the dangerous learning divide, with potentially negative consequences for the whole of society:

> Social cohesion, whereby a sense of solidarity and common interest binds a healthy society, is best engendered by education. As the economic need for a more highly educated and skilled workforce increases, the undereducated will fall even further behind than they are now. We

cannot risk increasing the gap between those with high skills, and those with low skills – or none at all. The uneducated will become disaffected and disenfranchised. Widespread alienation poses a threat to the stability of society. Education is not cheap, but ignorance carries high social and economic costs. (Committee of Vice-Chancellors and Principals cited in Fryer, 1997, 14)

Learning is perceived as a way of harnessing the potential talent of young people otherwise 'wasted in a vicious circle of under-achievement, self-deprecation, and petty crime'. The greatest challenge, therefore, is to break the cycle of poverty which profoundly affects so many communities and contributes to income inequality (DfEE, 1998, 11), and to change the culture in the many homes and workplaces where learning is not seen as having any relevance (p13).

Participation in lifelong learning within the discourse of individual responsibility is obligatory in the sense that the person, regardless of background or motivation, is expected to conform to this liberal principle of education as a kind of public duty to both self and state (Tight 1998b; Coffield 1999). Indeed, the onus of personal responsibility to invest in the new culture of learning is especially on under-represented people, such as the young disadvantaged. In other words, it is effectively those most disadvantaged through structural mechanisms who are expected to change themselves and get over whatever is bothering them.

Agency and the power to effect change

The policies construct learning as an imperative, and people as responsible for their own learning to ensure future success. That said, people effectively have 'agency without choice' because the interests of the individual and the interests of the state are seen as synonymous, and individual choices are impinged upon by the broader economic remit of government. However, the policies represent agency and individual responsibility in ways which suggest that the interests of the individual and the state are not necessarily the same, and conceivably at odds with each other. Individuals are urged to exercise agency and use lifelong learning to bring about change in society. The policies suggest that critical thinking and political activity are embedded in lifelong learning, and that democracy can be strengthened through participation in lifelong learning (Fryer, 1997, 17). Terms and phrases such as 'critical reflection', 'creative initiative', 'new forms of participation in politics' and 'self-activity, initiative and pluralism' are used (Fryer, 1997, 17). The argument put forward in Fryer's report is that education itself engenders choice, and enables people to be personally involved in constructing the kind of society they desire:

> If people and organisations are to influence economic and industrial change as well as respond to it, they need a range of skills, capacities and outlooks which will enable them to exercise choice for themselves. Lifelong learning can help people to seize new opportunities, engage critically with change and shape their worlds by asserting some ownership and direction over their lives, in work and beyond. (Fryer, 1997, 12)

> The personal and social damage inflicted by inequality, social exclusion and restricted opportunity is now widely recognised. Lifelong learning should represent a resource for people, and whole societies, to help them identify such inequalities, probe their origins and begin to challenge them, using skills, information and knowledge to achieve change. (Fryer, 1997, 17)

The policies display an unwavering commitment to the modernist principles of equality and social inclusion, and the power of the individual to effect change for the better. The current new liberal paradigm caters for all eventualities. The idea that continuous learning is inherently right underpins all the policy discourses. Therefore the government probably does not actually expect people to think outside the box and challenge normative ways of doing things. As for a feminist political project, it seems that emancipation from, and resistance to, dominant state discourses are severely limited. Critical thinking and political activity are fine as long as they remain inside the box. Although the government encourages reflexivity, it does not want any kind of reflexivity, but as Greener (2002) has argued, a 'reflexivity that accepts the existing rules of the game and attempts to make the best of them, rather than attempting to challenge the rules themselves' (p699). Therefore the only real emancipation can be from the existing rules of the game which form the basis of the universalistic and modernist state paradigm.

Concepts of personhood

This section examines how the selected policy documents construct their subjects, and who is excluded by these constructions. An overview of education policy over the last two decades reveals that although the proposition of education for all has remained central to education policy in Britain since the mid 1980s (DES, 1985; Fryer, 1997; DfEE, 1998, 1999), there has been a shift away from the culturally relativist position on personhood evident in the policies of the 1980s (DES, 1981, 1985), which referred to particular racial and cultural groups as encapsulating a definitive substantive content (Rattansi, 1992; Asad, 1993), towards an ever more individualistic discourse of personhood in which there is virtually no mention of race, ethnicity and culture. Education policies explicitly concerned with race and minority issues ceased after 1988, and the subject of race became what Apple (1999) has referred to as an 'absent presence' (p12). In recent policy, the individual has been represented as culturally neutral, and differences between people seen largely in terms of external socio-economic factors which can be overcome.

Whilst the policy documents under scrutiny here are thematically similar, their constructions of personhood revealed both similarities and differences. The concept of personhood in all the policy documents was underpinned by the wider government discourse of individualism. This concept combined elements of both economic and political liberalism, and portrayed the individual as rational, autonomous and utility-maximising. The assumption was that the person had the ability to increase productivity, develop personally, and empower her or himself through ever more learning, training and hard work, and thereby to continuously move closer to a complete self.

There was a marked difference between how the two earlier policy documents, *Learning for the Twenty-first Century* (Fryer, 1997) and *The Learning Age* (DfEE, 1998), and the most recent one, *Learning to Succeed* (DfEE, 1999), constructed personhood, despite only a year between them. The two earlier documents convey a halfway position between the culturally relativistic notion of personhood evident in the education policies of the 1980s (DES, 1981, 1985), and the wholly individualistic concept of personhood evident in *Learning to Succeed*.

In the two earlier documents, universalistic and individualistic notions of personhood sit comfortably with the idea that there are distinct groups of people who share certain characteristics. The claim in these documents is that policy development and lifelong learning strategies need to be targeted at particular sub-groups within the meta-group 'under-represented people'. These under-represented sub-groups include:

- disaffected young adults, notably young men
- older people
- people with learning difficulties and/or disabilities
- minority ethnic and linguistic groups
- prisoners and ex-offenders
- unskilled manual workers
- part-time and temporary workers
- people without qualifications, unemployed people
- some groups of women – notably lone parents
- those on the lowest incomes
- those living in remote or isolated areas
- people with literacy and/or numeracy difficulties (Fryer, 1997, 16).

Some of these groups of people and the obstacles they face are captured in a single paragraph in *Learning for the Twenty-first Century* (Fryer, 1997): other people's attitudes, the problem of stairs, and institutional regulations are all smoothly juxtaposed in a few short sentences:

> Older people often find the modern drive for certification gets in the way. Unemployed people are regularly deterred by the rigid application of benefit rules. Too often, Black and Asian people still experience institutional and personal racism. Other people's attitudes are a major barrier for people with learning difficulties; stairs too often limit choices for people in wheelchairs; and those with learning difficulties are too often confronted by a lack of suitable facilities or properly trained staff. (Fryer, 1997, 20)

The under-represented group 'minority ethnic and linguistic groups' is of most interest in this policy analysis. Fryer's report recognises that racial and ethnic cultures, religions, traditions and values should be reflected in provision for lifelong learning. It acknowledges that black people get less opportunity to study at their employers' expense, and older people from black and Asian communities are especially disadvantaged; moreover, 500,000 people for whom English is a second language experience particular difficulties (Basic Skills Agency cited in Fryer, 1997, 63-64).

Whereas Fryer's report makes general reference to black and Asian people, the subsequent policy *The Learning Age* (DfEE, 1998) distinguishes between different groups of black and Asian people, and acknowledges that there is a need to identify why some people such as Bangladeshi women and African-Caribbean men, as well as women in certain academic disciplines, remain under-represented (DfEE, 1998, 51). This policy concern corresponds with research published a year later highlighting the under-achievement of working-class African-Caribbean boys (Arnot *et al*, 1999), which constituted a moral panic in the late 1990s and was referred to as a crisis in masculinity (Lucey and Walkerdine, 1999). It also correlates with later research which showed that Bangladeshi and Pakistani women and African-Caribbean men were less likely to be studying at university (*Social Trends* 30, 2000: 56 cited in Tomlinson, 2001, 147). However, there is little information in the policy documents about why these groups are under-represented and what might be undertaken, other than 'creating a culture of learning', to solve the problems.

Readers of the policy documents might be forgiven for believing that there is something distinctive about being Asian, black, Bangladeshi or African-Caribbean which leads to their under-representation within the education system. There is no discussion of the problems faced by ethnic minority people, such as discrimination, institutional racism and low self-expectations, and the effect this may have on their educational experiences. The same applies to other under-represented people such as ex-offenders, lone parents, old people and people with learning difficulties. These people are portrayed as being on the wrong side of the learning divide and lacking qualifications and skills, which suggests notions of disadvantage, dependency, low self-expectation, 'poverty, low status, lack of self-esteem and powerlessness' (Fryer, 1997, 16).

The final part of this chapter looks more closely at the most recent policy text *Learning to Succeed* (DfEE, 1999). In contrast to the other two policy documents, this document makes virtually no reference to ethnic minority groups. A word search revealed that no results were obtained for the words black, Asian, ethnic minority/minorities, and there was no reference to any established categories of personhood apart from 'young people', which was referred to 113 times. One result was obtained for ethnic groups, which appeared in the appendix (DfEE, 1999, 76). The words race, disability and gender were also used only once, all in one sentence, and concerned the issue of widening access: 'particularly for those people who face disadvantage in the labour market because of their race, disability, gender or age' (DfEE, 1999, 28). The absence of these terms in the policy documents is at odds with the social science literature around education which shows that race, gender and class potentially have a profound effect on people's lives and educational experiences (Ball *et al*, 2000; Reay, 2000; Archer *et al*, 2003).

The phrase older people appeared five times, learning difficulties five times, disabilities ten times, and disabled three times. The term culture was referred to four times, but only in the context of creating a new 'culture of learning'. The words poverty, poor and class yielded no results in the context of persons.

People were referred to as disadvantaged eleven times. Here are some examples of how the term was used: 'promoting equality of opportunity and ensuring that the needs of the most disadvantaged in the labour market are best met' (DfEE, 1999, 24); 'ensure targeted support for the socially disadvantaged' (p34); 'target more specific help on the most disadvantaged where specific financial obstacles act as a real barrier to participation (p50). The document also juxtaposed the disadvantaged with people who experience other types of difficulties. For example, it referred to: 'the socially disadvantaged or those who otherwise lack confidence'; 'socially disadvantaged and disabled people' (DfEE, 1999, 58); the voluntary sector as 'understanding the needs of the disadvantaged and excluded' (p40); 'disadvantaged young people and helping those at most risk of dropping out' (p42); the system as 'failing a significant section of the community, often the most vulnerable and disadvantaged' (p16). Again, there is no explanation about who the disadvantaged are, and what is meant by the various terms used within the context of disadvantage.

References to under-represented people are made in easily identifiable categorical terms, such as minority ethnic and linguistic groups, lone mothers, young people, people with learning difficulties, and the disadvantaged. These groups of people are represented as possessing distinctive and fixed features. Yet elsewhere the policy, as we have seen, also conceptualises individuals as inherently flexible and adaptable, with limitless potential to change themselves and society. The policy constructions therefore reflect individualist and essentialist discourses of selfhood, as well as the postmodern discourse in which identity may be constantly transformed.

The concepts of personhood identified in the three policy documents draw attention to the *impasse* in the context of mixed heritage identity highlighted in Chapter Two: how to create inclusion without resorting to either individualism or essentialist categories. In the field of education the difficulty centres on how to reconcile an inclusive universal education system with identity specific needs.

So far this analysis of the policy documents has looked at the stories being presented in the documents in terms of the discourses used and how they reflected trends in society, and at ideas and categories around social exclusion and inclusion. It has also looked at how the policy documents differed in their concepts of personhood and how the texts constructed their subjects as learners. The next chapter examines what the women in this study said about their experiences of education, and what they thought about the government and education policy discourses analysed in this chapter.

7

Reflections on Further Education

This chapter focuses on what the interviews revealed about education. It compares what the women said about their experiences of education and the opinions they gave on education policy discourses, with the discourses from the previous chapter to show how the women positioned themselves in relation to these government and education policy discourses. The interview questions arose out of wider discourses around education and the discourses identified in the policy documents, such as the value of education, learning for economic and personal reward, instilling a culture of learning, equality of opportunity, social inclusion, and individual responsibility (Fryer, 1997; DfEE, 1998, 1999). The chapter begins by examining what the women said about their choice of course and the college they attended, their plans for the future, and whether they thought they had had the same chances as everyone else in education. It goes on to explore the women's views on government and policy discourses around education, such as what constitutes a good education, whether people can learn to want to learn, and what they think about inclusion and exclusion.

This survey is of predominantly working-class women. Some educationalists have asked why, despite extensive government initiatives to widen participation, students from working-class backgrounds are still not as successful at school as middle-class students, and why they still mainly go on to working-class occupations. Bourdieu (1977) argued that the education system works as a reproduction strategy for the dominant group, structured to favour those who have cultural capital.

Schools, for example, take on the *habitus* of the dominant class, and this sets the standards for academic success (Bourdieu and Passeron, 1977).

The concept of *habitus* is central to Bourdieu's theories. According to this theory, cultural knowledge is transmitted by the families of each social class, and is absorbed and internalised through successive generations. This creates the *habitus*, which is made up of dominant ways of thinking, concepts and categories which have been built up from early experiences and hard-wired into people's self-beliefs, thoughts, and ways of behaving. This initial sense of self is reinforced throughout life and is resistant to change; the *habitus* therefore has the power to reproduce social situations. A person's *habitus* engenders a sense of limits which determines the degree of their success and failure. This means that transformations in people's educational aspirations may be difficult, and policy objectives, such as creating a love of learning or increasing the participation of under-represented people, are exposed as simplistic and short-sighted.

Whilst acknowledging that agents are not passive players within dominant discourses but are actively engaged in 'individual and collective self-making and sense-making' (Delhi, 1996 cited in Reay, 2000), Reay *et al* (2001) have suggested that the educational choices made by young people parallel their unequal access to cultural, social and economic capital. Working-class people position themselves within the middle-class discourses of the 'market and individual reliance' which are seldom chosen by working-class people themselves (Reay, 2000, 994). They have limited choice and can either accept a 'spoilt identity' (Reay and Ball, 1997) or, as is increasingly happening, reject the label working-class (Skeggs, 1997).

The complexity of the processes involved in young working-class people making choices in education is evident in the growing literature in this field (Maguire *et al*, 1999; Ball *et al*, 2000; Foskett and Hemsley-Brown, 2001). Environmental factors, the familial, social and institutional contexts, and the circumstances around daily experiences are all significant (Ball *et al*, 2000). Some researchers have argued that in making choices young people take the path of least resistance by either staying on at school or following a path which is the norm for their socio-economic group (Foskett *et al*, 2003). Asian students, for example, are more likely to follow professional career paths, which may be related to the entrepreneurial concerns of their parents (Mirza, 1992).

Experiences of education
Choices and experiences of courses and colleges

The women in this study were asked: *Why did you choose this college and the course you are doing?* Over half of them (21) said they had chosen the college because of its location, which usually meant its proximity to their homes or workplaces. This underlines the government policy objective that FE colleges should serve local communities, and explains why these colleges have survived. Social reasons for choice of college were also frequent – because friends were studying there, or the college had been recommended by friends, or because they wanted to meet people from different backgrounds. A few women said they wanted to go *'somewhere different'*. Danielle (English/Jamaican) *'wanted to jump in at the deep end'*, and Lekeisha ('fully mixed'), who travelled over an hour from north London to east London every day, said she chose the college because she *'liked the facade'*. One woman said she chose the college because it had childcare facilities. Three respondents said that they had chosen the college because it was the only one offering the course they wanted to do, and another three that they had had no choice in coming to that particular college.

Almost half the women said that the course they had chosen had been a means to an end, to get a particular job, career or qualification. Around two thirds of the women (24 in all) said they had experienced no problems with the course or college and gave positive feedback. Most said they had learned many new things or that it was a good course, and students who were doing hairdressing, beauty, fashion or art courses, often used words such as *'like'*, *'enjoy'* or *'interesting'* to describe their courses.

The women were asked whether the course they were doing was vocational or academic. Nearly all replied that they were doing an academic course, although the vast majority of them were doing a vocational course. This was probably because of the government's conflation of the academic and the vocational, in which vocational qualifications are given an academic 'sheen', such as the new vocational A-levels and vocational GCSEs (Mizen, 2003, 460), which has led to confusion about the status of qualifications. This supports Raggatt and Williams's (1999) observation that status is attached to academic qualifications and not vocational ones in our culture. It also echoes the findings of a study of two secondary schools in southern England: although students knew the difference between academic and vocational qualifications, they believed that any kind of degree course, regardless of content, was better than following a vocational education and training route (Killeen *et al*, 1999).

The women were also asked: *What have the positive aspects of the course been?* Around a quarter of the sample talked about their college education as worthwhile and as potentially opening doors, without being specific about why they had chosen particular courses. A similar theme was observed in a study by Francis (1999a), in which secondary school students' discussions of post-compulsory education reflected a discourse of the importance of being educated *per se*, without any explanation of why it was so important. Siham (Eritrean/Egyptian, GNVQ Business Studies) said that her qualification might get her a better job, but that the main reason for studying was '*because I just wanted to do something*', whilst Peta (African/West Indian-English, NVQ Childcare, Ex-FE) said that her qualification was '*another notch in my belt, something to fall back on*', although she was now doing something completely different. Chantel (English/African, ABC Advanced Business Studies) said:

> I needed a course which would take me onto a career path where I would have more options. There are things I love more than this course but because it opens more doors, this is a money world and I want some of it.

The women's main idea was that education was an investment for future reward. These views are supported by the government discourse of the value of education and the policy discourse of learning as an investment for reward, which is explored further in the next section on the women's vision of their futures.

Some women also talked about how their choice of course had been influenced by the need for a positive personal change. Rosa (Angolan-Portuguese/Portuguese, B-Tech Hairdressing) said she '*needed a complete change from working with mentally handicapped people to give me time to myself and catch my breath'*. Dianne (Welsh/Mauritian, A-Level Law, Media, Psychology) had planned to do a performing arts course and then decided to study law instead *'because I wanted to change my whole identity as a person'* and have a chance to *'find myself*. Kim (African [Cuban-Jamaican]/English, Access to HE Psychology) liked the fact that she now had *'routine and order. I haven't had to think, everything is planned for me and I only have to turn up and work.'* Chantel felt studying had forced her *'to be more intelligent because you have to use your brain'*.

Four students said they had had no choice about which course to study. All of them were doing basic level 1 courses. Cerisse (Scottish-African/ Zambian-English), a 16 year-old recent immigrant, had to do a summer course which prepared her for GCSEs. Cassandra's (Jamaican/Irish, Certificate in Skills for Working Life) course had been chosen for her by her school to help her with basic numeracy and literacy. Latesha (English/Jamaican, Certificate in Skills for Working Life) was on a course chosen by her school teacher. She said:

> I don't want to do anything. After school I wanted to stay at home and look after my brother, and get a Saturday job, but my mum wanted me to have better grades than I did so she said I had to go to college.

Lesley (Bajan/Scottish, NVQ New Directions) was doing the only course available to her, a basic vocational course, because she had failed the entry test for GCSEs. She expressed her anger about this:

> How the hell do they expect you to improve if they're going to be like that – I had no preparation and I'd been out of school and not done anything for a year. I didn't have a choice. I don't know if I'll pass [the course]. I don't know where I'll be in a year.

The women were also asked: *Have you experienced any problems with the course?* Only a few women said they had, and mentioned personal problems such as being too tired after work (Anabel, Guyanese/Indian-White), failing courses (Sumaira, Pakistani/English), or having difficulties with assignments (Jennifer, Caribbean-Portuguese-Asian/English-Irish) or exams (Dianne, Welsh/Mauritian). Management problems were also mentioned: timetables got mixed up and tutors failed to turn up (Asha, Jamaican/Irish-English), and the college had a *'bad attitude to students'* because it did not keep them informed about changes (Nadine, Iraqi/English). Lesley (Bajan/Scottish) said she had not received the support she needed, and Peta (African/West Indian-English) had left her course because she had a *'weak tutor'.*

The main obstacles to learning mentioned in the policy documents were not experienced by the women in this study. None of the respondents expressed any worries about the 'simple physical problems of the time, costs, location, range and accessibility of learning opportunities'; none of them talked about the 'absence of childcare, transport arrangements and even course times which may not fit in with collecting children from school' (Fryer Report, 1997, 20). This finding is not surprising because the respondents were all education users: a sample of non-users of FE may have yielded different results.

The findings in this section show that most of the women were studying in FE because they wanted to, and that only a few students in the 16 to 19 age range felt that they had no choice, or had problems with the courses they were studying. This challenges Furlong and Cartmel's (1997) supposition that top-down educational policies have created 'an army of reluctant conscripts to post-compulsory education' amongst 16 to 19 years olds (p17). The findings also differ from Fergusson *et al's* (2000) study which showed that over three quarters of the sample were in further education by default or because they were badly informed. These discrepancies in the research suggest that further investigation into mixed heritage and black people's choices and experiences of FE is needed.

Futures: '*As long as you're happy ...*'

Most of the women were asked about how they saw their future. I hoped to gain insight into the correlations between course choice, educational and career trajectories, and whether they believed they would fulfil their ambitions. The five ex-FE students who were working at the time of the interview, Anisha, Brenda, Peta, Tania and Ruby, are not included in this section, although it is interesting that two of these women had jobs which were unrelated to the qualifications they had gained. The questions asked were: *How do you see your future? Do you think you will have the skills and qualifications you need to do that/get there?*

All the women said they were working towards a specific objective, and nearly all of them said that they were positive about gaining the qualifications and skills they needed in order to reach their objective. However, two thirds of them were simultaneously unsure about their future and had no clear vision of where they would be or what they would be doing. This supports the idea that young people's learning careers do not accord with rational planning, but 'happen' or 'unfold' (Bloomer, 1997, 153), and may be experienced as states of liminality in which future employment is seen as unclear (Bettis, 1996 cited in Archer and Yamashita, 2003a).

The notion that the future is indeterminate is echoed in literature on students' post-16 trajectories. Drawing on research on 16 to 19 year-olds, Fergusson *et al* (2000) claimed that: 'Movement seems opportunistic rather than purposive. It is characterised by *ad hoc*, multiple and diverse experiences rather than any semblance of 'career' ... It is a system in which inclusion is assured, but outcome is uncertain' (p295). In a study of working-class people's participation in HE, Archer *et al* (2003) showed that respondents believed that a university degree would enhance their employment prospects, but also that there were considerable risks attached to postgraduate employment because the employment market was overcrowded.

The women's responses all reflected the policy discourse of learning as an investment for personal reward or development. Many intimated that something, even if it was not a good job, would come out of education, such as making you a better person, or making you happy. Some women said that the purpose of education was to bring greater happiness, and that this was more important than following a specific career path. All the women quoted below intended to go to university:

> As long as you're happy it doesn't matter whether you get a good job at the end of it – I'd rather be happy and pot-less. Nadine (Iraqi/English, Art Foundation)

> I try not to think about the future too much, just let things happen, whatever life brings really. I see my qualification as leading me to something happy, it doesn't matter what I do as long as I'm happy. Dianne (Welsh/Mauritian, A-Level Law, Media, Psychology)

It's about doing something good, something I've worked and qualified on ... but the main thing is being happy with what you're doing, so I might even change my mind about what I'm doing now. Adriana (Angolan-Portuguese/Angolan, Access to HE Law)

Several women talked about their future in terms of dreams. This theme was also observed in a study by Archer and Yamashita (2003a). The idea that education is an imperative compels people to take up educational opportunities and 'aim high'. Some of the women talked about their aspirations as dreams and as unrealistic.

My dream was always to be a translator, but I also just want a job – nothing special just something that can make me independent, and be happy with my daughter. Olga (Italian/Eritrean, EFL)

My dream is to be a forensic scientist, but I'm not good at science, so a police officer will do. Paula (Romanian/Greek, Diploma in Public Services)

The most important thing is to fulfil your dreams. I don't know what I want to do, maybe medicine or science, so I've chosen something enjoyable first. Jennifer (Caribbean-Portuguese-Asian/English-Irish, NVQ in Beauty Therapy)

I have no idea! I dream too much. University would obviously be the ideal, but I can't know for sure. Chantel (ABC Advanced Business Studies)

Some women who were studying for level 1 or 2 qualifications talked about embarking on long and arduous educational careers, yet also had get-out clauses in case they failed. Hodkinson *et al's* (2000) notion of 'horizons for action' is a useful concept for understanding these women's positions (p358). It allows for the incorporation of both static and fluid elements of a person: choices are made within horizons of action, in which people take measures to maximise their chances of success and also minimise their sense of failure. Cassandra (Jamaican/Irish, Certificate in Skills for Working Life), who had difficulties with basic numeracy and literacy, was studying for a level 1 qualification and wanted to become a primary school teacher. She did not know whether she would gain the necessary qualifications to become a teacher, but that if she didn't, it would be because she had changed her mind about what she wanted to do. Nichole (three quarters Black/a quarter White, Basic Maths), who was also studying on a level 1 course, wanted to become a reception teacher: if she failed, she said, it would be because of competition. Nichole charted her educational route:

> I then need to do GCSEs, A-levels, an Access course, then a degree, and then a PGCE. It's a long, long process. But I need to do this or I'll stay a nursery nurse for the next 40 years ... If I don't get anywhere, it won't be because I'm not good enough, but because competition is so fierce.

Only one woman, Lianne (St. Lucian/English, NVQ Catering), expressed any cynicism about learning as an investment for reward, and talked about the problem of qualification inflation. Ainley (1994) has argued that the meritocratic link between the qualifications gained and employment opportunities become increasingly untenable as people feel obligated to get more and more education. Lianne said *'they've got their degree but are working in awful jobs and it hasn't taken them anywhere'*, and contended that the government should take responsibility for making false promises.

The findings on respondents' futures, although limited in scope, reflect the government's emphasis on individual responsibility to take up the educational opportunities on offer, and so give a people a sense that they are investing in futures of their own choosing (Peters, 1996). The women drew on personal development and quality of life discourses to evoke the idea that education was useful in itself, and possibly to cover their backs in case they failed in the employment market. The findings accord with Warmington's (2002) study of mature students' participation in Access to HE courses, which showed that students justified going along with the government's agenda by choosing to view education as personal insurance.

Any ambivalence or uncertainty about respondents' futures, whether articulated in terms of happiness, dreams or excessive aspirations, can be understood within the framework of the government discourses of economic efficiency and personal development which are central to the policy documents discussed in Chapter Six (Fryer, 1997; DfEE, 1998, 1999).

Reflections on policy discourses
The value of education: '*Education is better than silver and gold*'

Respondents were asked: *What does a good education mean to you?* The aim was to compare the ideas put forward in the policy documents about the value of education with the women's opinions on this subject. Most of them viewed education as good in itself, and as providing a range of different purposes and functions. A good education was seen as an investment for instrumental reward, including economic and material reward and personal reward.

Around half the sample said that a good education depended on good support and access, including a '*good teacher*', '*good facilities*', '*good resources*', '*equality of opportunity*' and '*access to opportunity*'. In instrumentalist terms, a good education was about getting '*good grades*' or '*the right qualifications*', a '*good job*', a '*better job*' or a '*job you want to do*', and for '*getting somewhere in life*'. Over half the respondents reflected the policy discourse of meritocracy, and said that those with a higher level of education had a better chance of getting a good job. Nichole's (three quarters Black/a quarter White) response was typical: '*If you don't study then you don't get that prize job at the end of it.*' These findings support the discourses discussed in Chapter Six (Fryer, 1997; DfEE, 1998, 1999) in which a direct link is made between lifelong learning, an economically competitive society, personal success and individual responsibility.

Many respondents reproduced both instrumentalist and personal development discourses in their discussions about what constituted a good education, and some drew only on the personal development discourse. In this sense, their views differed from those of the students in Killeen *et al*'s (1999) study, who adopted a wholly instrumentalist view of education, in which qualifications could be directly exchanged for employment opportunities. Francis's (1999a) study of school students' opinions on post-compulsory education also revealed that an unequivocal link was made between academic attainment and future job prospects.

Life skills such as eclecticism, adaptability and happiness in feeling that they were more rounded individuals were as important for many of the women in the study as a job or a career. This amalgamation of the functional and personal benefits of education is supported by the discourse of the liberal individual as an 'unfinished' self perpetually striving for completion. Here are some responses which demonstrate a combination of instrumentalist and personal development discourses in describing a good education:

> Good job, good prospects and a good life, and being independent and confident, a good grounding basically. It's part of the whole *persona*, it's very, very important. Peta (African/West Indian-English, NVQ Childcare, Ex-FE)

> ... not only to get a job, but I want to do it for myself, yeah, I think it's important to learn as much as you can while you still have the brainpower, and you can still get a good job from it. Lekeisha ('Fully mixed', NVQ Hairdressing)

> ... getting everything that you want, doing everything that you want to do, finding out things for you. Emma (Jamaican/English, GNVQ Art and Design)

The notion of education for life was also evident:

> It's not just about getting the grades, it's about having the understanding and applying it to life because that is the whole point. Ella (A-Levels Psychology, Biology, Business, Media)

> It's the most important thing in life, and it should come first before any other thing. Paula (Romanian/Greek, Diploma Public Services)

> My parents told me that education is something no one can ever take away from you. That is what it means to me. Keira ('AS' Levels Government, Politics, Law, History)

However, Kerry (English/Bajan, B-Tech Performing Arts), succinctly pointed out that: '*Education itself is not the key, it plays a big part in people's lives but it's what you do with it that matters.*'

The older students and those who had completed their FE studies emphasised self-development and played down the instrumentalist aspect of education. Their narratives strongly reflected a humanist discourse in which a direct link was made between the value of education and becoming a better person. The responses are reminiscent of what

Foucault has referred to as subjectification, in which the individual is constructed as a self-surveying acting subject who seeks self-know-ledge (Rabinow, 1986), and is invited to take part in the quest to get to know her or himself better. For Ruby (Punjabi Indian/Irish, Legal Exe-cutive Certificate, Ex-FE), a good education involved her search for her own identity:

> The education I've received in my life has been much more than just about my formal education. I feel I've been very much educated by other people looking for their own identity. It's about sharing experiences, I think that's been a really key thing, and to have access to as many opportunities and as much information, to be well-supported and have people believe in you and your abilities.

For Anabel (Guyanese/Indian-White), who had a degree and was taking a computer course, learning could open the door to fuller understand-ing:

> Education is better than silver and gold – that is something that has been instilled in me, learning is the key, the only thing that can unlock you from ignorance. And I mean it's not a case of having an education to earn loads of money, it's that freedom from ignorance, and yes, so, you liberate yourself so that you can grow and spring in different directions, whereas without an education it's just like you are sunk in a pit that you can't come out from.

The prospect of greater economic materialism was a significant motiva-tion behind acquiring an education for many of the women. For others, following Beck and Beck-Gernsheim (2001) the 'conventional symbols of success (income, career, status) no longer fulfil their need for self-dis-covery and self-assertion or their hunger for a 'fuller life" (p38). There-fore the women's views on what constitutes a good education are con-sistent with the view that material sacrifices are bearable if they are accompanied by a guaranteed increase in self-development (Beck and Beck-Gernsheim, 2001, 162). It seems likely that as more and more people are university educated, and qualifications progressively lose their value, that 'duty to oneself' to take up the educational oppor-tunities on offer will increasingly co-exist with the idea that happiness is more important than education for material ends, work or status.

Most of the women talked about the benefits of education in purely individual terms, not in collective terms. Few women reflected the policy view that education should profit both the individual and the whole of society (Fryer, 1997; DfEE, 1998, 1999). Whilst Kim (African [Cuban-Jamaican]/English, Access to HE Psychology) saw a good education as something which would enable her to have '*the house, the car, the holiday*', it was also about '*stimulating your brain*' and about doing things '*that will benefit other people and help them be productive*'. The alternative for Kim was being '*at the mercy of what telly puts into your head*'.

Frida (Colombian/Polish Jewish-English, A-Levels: Politics, History, English Literature) believed that education was to enable people to think analytically, and was a prerequisite for the broader political project of equality and justice. A good education was an important aspect of identity: it opened up possibilities for alternative and independent ways of thinking which could impact on the choices an individual would feel were available to them. Frida's views reflected the discourse of social inclusion: she was the only respondent who referred to the issue of agency and the power of the individual to effect the wider change in society which was identified in the policy documents. A good education for Frida was

> Something that helps you to think, be analytical, be able to act and take decisions that will help you to be independent. It should be able to give you the ability to act in a way that sort of enables you to deepen democracy and make society a fairer place, in the sense that people have more control. Education and control are linked quite a lot, control over one's life, one's future, one's decisions. I suppose it's choice, which doesn't imply that education actually does that at the present moment, or the education that I've had has done that, but that's what I think is a good education.

Tania (West Indian/English, B-Tech in Support and Foundation in Counselling Skills) also saw a good education as part of a wider political project, but her articulations drew on both the discourses of social inclusion and economic efficiency. Unlike Frida, who believed that independent thinking was essential for creating a more egalitarian society, Tania argued that a cohesive nuclear family structure was the cornerstone of both the 'rounded individual' and an economically competitive society.

> A good education would bring out the best in people, would enable a person to know themselves, what their strengths and weaknesses are. People should be educated in morality, relationships, parenting, forgiveness, discipline – if the government wants an economic society it has to deal with the root of the problem which means building a secure society through reviving family structure.

These findings reveal that a good education was understood by the women in functional instrumentalist terms, and in terms of its potential for personal development. They support the government discourse of the value of education, and the policy discourse of investing in learning for economic and personal reward, discussed in Chapter Six (Fryer, 1997; DfEE, 1998, 1999). Learning was understood as something which was good in itself and had no disadvantages. In this sense, the women unquestioningly bought into the idea that the interests of the state and the individual, as the joint beneficiaries of education, are merged: the nation benefits from better educated and skilled individuals, and the individual benefits from incremental material prosperity and a sense of personal fulfilment.

Equal opportunities and self-responsibility: 'It's there if you want it, you just got to go and get it'

In the interview questions, the women were asked: *Do you feel you have had the same chances as everyone else in education?* A related question was: *In its further education policy the government talks about being inclusive of all people. Do you think that everyone is equally included in education?* The vast majority of respondents believed that they were the beneficiaries of an egalitarian education system. This view is underpinned by the discourse of equality of opportunity.

Whilst most of the women believed that their choices were largely unfettered and that they had had the same chances in education as everyone else, over three quarters of the sample simultaneously said that there were specific groups of people who were not equally included in education. One quarter of the sample identified '*poor people*' and another quarter said that '*disabled people*' or '*people with special needs*' were not equally included in education. Five women said race or colour were sometimes problematic issues in terms of inclusion. However, whilst social background and personal circumstances might impede other people's choices to get an education, most of the women saw themselves as exempt from such constrictions. In claiming that they were equally included in education, but that poor people and people with learning difficulties were not, the women were making a distinction between themselves and marginalised others by means of a dependency/independency dichotomy: they saw themselves as making choices independently about their lives and their futures, in contrast to the supposed dependence of those unable or unwilling to help themselves.

The women's discussions around who was not equally included in education were also produced by the discourse of social inclusion, in which certain groups are seen as marginalised in society and in need of being brought into the mainstream learning culture. However, their responses were at odds with the policy document *Learning to Succeed* (DfEE, 1999) which was scanned for its references to categories of personhood, and found to make no references to poor people or poverty, and only some references to disability and people with learning difficulties. Conversely, none of the women mentioned 'disadvantaged people' despite the 113 references to this generic group in the policy document. The policy text barely made any references to race, culture, ethnicity or gender. In alluding to specific and traditional categories rather than the universal meta-categories used in the policies, the women reflected popular, as opposed to policy, discourses around marginalised people in education.

Many women thought that disadvantages in education could be overcome. Alongside the discourses of equality of opportunity and social inclusion, they drew on the discourse of individual responsibility. The dominant view on education was 'it's there if you want it'. Asha (Jamaican/Irish-English, B-Tech Beauty Therapy) said bluntly: '*Everyone has the chance to learn but not everyone wants to take the opportunity to learn, but it is there for everyone.*'

Petra (African/Portuguese), who was studying for a GNVQ in Foundation Science, and wanted to be a doctor or a therapist, said that anyone could go to college provided they put their mind to it:

> At the end of the day it's their choice to be someone – if they don't want to do it you can't force 'em. If they want to be here they have to work hard. If they don't want to be here it's because they don't want to use their brains.

Whilst recognising that some people such as mature students and single mothers might find going into further education *'quite hard to wangle,'* Nadine (Iraqi/English) said that the important thing was *'to want it enough – it shouldn't be so easy that anyone can do it willy-nilly and take advantage.'* Dianne (Welsh/Mauritian) asserted that *'even disability has special schools, and overseas scholarships give everyone globally the chance to study.'* Kim (African [Cuban-Jamaican]/English) pointed out that of the 30 women who started her course, most of whom were single mothers, and only two had no children, only fifteen women were left. According to Kim this was not a problem of childcare, cost or timetabling, as the course was designed for people with children, but a problem of personal motivation. For her, the responsibility lay with the individual:

> Despite the daily problems, it's down to you to get the work done. You have to really want to do it, you have to help yourself. But it will be hard, and that scares a lot of people ... The only people that won't be educated are those who can't be bothered and have to work in menial jobs.

Only six respondents said that they had not had the same chances as everyone else in education, or that they had not had the education they would have liked. All of them felt that not everyone was equally included in education. Only two first generation women felt that they had not had the same chances as everyone else in education. Lesley's (Bajan/Scottish) quote encapsulates notions of self-responsibility, possessing innate intelligence, and the responsibility of the education provider:

> Yes, definitely at school, but I messed up big time, I could have worked better. Some teachers had faith in me but I had a lot of boy trouble. I was on my own – me and my friends we'd bunk lessons and that, but they was a lot cleverer than me, a lot cleverer, and they still got their GCSEs, even though they got a D or a C. Here I haven't had the same chances cos they didn't let me do my GCSEs.

Ruby, a first generation Punjabi Indian/Irish woman in her forties, described her experiences at school in the 1970s as a mixture of discrimination, low self-esteem and low self-expectations, and a lack of agency about decisions about her schooling. Part of her early education had been at an approved school, a place she believed she was sent due to the ignorance which prevailed at that time about people who were trans-racially adopted. Ruby said that having the *'opportunity to go on to FE was the best thing that ever happened to me'*.

Four out of the six women who felt they were not equally included in education were second generation or multiple heritage women whose racial heritage was predominantly black. It was significant that, apart from Jasmine (Grenadian-Scottish/Dominican), they had all overcome their barriers to learning, and drew on the discourses of equality of opportunity and individual responsibility in their assertion that 'education is there if you want it'. Not being educated was ultimately seen as a choice and an act of self-exclusion, and not due to external or structural factors.

Nichole's (three quarters Black/a quarter White, Basic Maths) quotes show how the discourses of social inclusion, equality of opportunity and individual responsibility may all be drawn on at the same time. Nichole had experienced *'few advantages in life and had to struggle to become a nursery nurse.'* In the past she had questioned why she had not had the same chances as everyone else, but had decided that there were no barriers to achievement, and that it was down to her to get over her own internalised colour barrier:

> I used to wonder why I found it hard to get jobs, whether it was the colour of my skin or something else, but now I know I can go out there ... [now I] think that all I need to do is get on with life and not let the colour barrier come into it because you won't achieve anything.

> It's up to you. I don't think there are any barriers, it's there if you want it, you just got to go and get it. It would be harder if you have dependants but you have to make some sacrifices to get what you want, and some people aren't prepared to do that.

Anabel (Guyanese/Indian-White), who was a teacher in her forties, also said that she had not always had the same chances as everyone else.

The discrimination she had experienced from lecturers on her degree course '*was so overt I really felt that I stuck out like a sore thumb*', and she said she had had '*to work extra hard*' to get her degree. Work colleagues, on the other hand, were always supportive '*even though they were all white*'. Anabel also drew on the discourses of inclusion, equality of opportunity and individual responsibility in suggesting that '*denied opportunities*' were not because of institutional failings, but because of the choices young people themselves made:

> I don't know why people have been denied opportunities, maybe they themselves have contributed to why those opportunities were not offered to them. It could be to do with attitudes to learning, where it's all about getting rich quick – every teenager now wants to be a pop-star or a model. So they think why must I go four years and study hard at university and struggle on a grant and come out with a debt of how many thousand pounds?

Jasmine (Grenadian-Scottish/Dominican, GCSE Humanities) was emphatic about not having had the same chances as everyone else, and said that she still experienced discrimination in education today. Her talk did not reproduce the discourses of equality of opportunity and individual responsibility. She did, however, express the view that discrimination was due to the behaviour of individuals, and not the responsibility of government or institutions. Jasmine had attended a secondary school with only black students, but because of incessant bullying left school before sitting her GCSEs; the same thing had happened at college and she had failed her exams as a result. Jasmine felt that because she did not speak slang like the black people in her class that '*they think I think I'm too good for them.*' She was incredulous that '*acting white*' was seen as synonymous with being intelligent:

> Black people won't talk to you if you show knowledge or intelligence. The other day I was talking to a boy and he was like – you're so white, you act like white people – and I'm like, just because you see an intelligent black person in front of you that means they're acting white? I'm like, to be black and to be intelligent, that means you're trying to act white?

> It's not the government's fault, but the individual's fault, because people discriminate against each other – the college is very strict on the race thing and stops it to a certain extent. It's people's fault why it happens.

> One of my really big problems is how to be included – inclusivity doesn't work for me. Everything reverts back to discrimination.

Nalia (three quarters Black/a quarter Chinese, NVQ Administration) was one of the few respondents who made any reference to class differences and unequal chances in education, claiming *'I've probably had the same chances as other working-class people, but not the same chances as upper-class people.'* Of the four women discussed here, Nalia was the only one who said that people's exclusion was due to institutional flaws. On whether she felt everyone was equally included in education, she said:

> Not really, no. They try but it's hard. Some people have the ability but they still fall through the net. Attention is mostly given to those that do want to learn, and that's hard enough, and others just get ignored.

The issue of 'institutional and personal racism' referred to in *Learning for the Twenty-first Century* (Fryer, 1997) was talked about by only a few women. None of the women talked specifically about institutional or personal racism, and tended to use the term 'discrimination'. Jasmine was the only woman in the sample who specifically said she currently experienced personal racism in her educational life. Anabel and Ruby both said that institutional discrimination had affected their educational lives in the past. Only a few women referred to race and cultural issues generally within institutions. Nichole, who had expected a totally mixed class at college, said that she was *'shocked that the course consisted mainly of white people, and five token black, and five token Asians!'* Frida (Columbian/Polish Jewish-English) commented on being troubled by the division she observed between Asian and white students at the college she had attended a few years before.

The discourses of equality of opportunity and self-responsibility for learning were palpable in that most of the women believed that personal success was down to motivation and commitment. The findings also reflect the education policy view that people who do not participate in education are responsible for changing their own behaviour, and that non-participation inevitably leads to exclusion. The findings support the observation made by Ball *et al* (2000) that young people see themselves as individuals in a meritocratic setting, and not as classed members of an unequal society. The danger is that people can become pathologised through such discourses. Social inequalities are explained away by individual disposition and social problems are increasingly understood in terms of personal psychological inadequacies which are no longer seen as being rooted in the social realm (Beck and Beck-Gernsheim, 2001). The next section illustrates not only that many of the women thought that people should be responsible for their own learning, but that there must also be a predisposition towards learning in the first place.

Learning to learn: *'It has to come from within'*

The women were asked: *Do you think people can learn to want to learn?* This question elicited the opinions of 28 respondents on how they saw other people's attitudes towards education and learning. The question related to the policy discourse of lifelong learning and specifically to the government's policy objective of creating a culture of learning (Fryer, 1997; DfEE, 1998). Its purpose was to gain insight into how the women viewed possible constraints on people's aspirations and participation in education.

Responses correlated with the findings above on equality of opportunity and self-responsibility in education, that 'education is there if you want it, you just got to go and get it'. Personal motivation was understood to be behind success in learning, and this depended on a person's innate predisposition to learning. The theme of innate predisposition did not correspond directly with any of the policy discourses or wider discourses around education but supported the humanist position on selfhood discussed in Chapter Two.

Several women said that the will to learn had to *'come from within'*, and was attributable to individual personality. According to Chantel (English/African), basic resources should be available, but that it was down to the individual: *'If you want to learn you will learn. You can help, but it has to come from within.'* Kerry (English/Bajan) argued that the propensity to learn *'has to be there from the beginning, from day one'*, and added *'it's a lot to do with yourself – either you get on or you don't ... some people will never change'*. Like Kerry, Kim (African [Cuban-Jamaican]/English) believed that some people would never change. The birth of her daughter had turned her towards education, and whilst

130

she was succeeding in education through her own personal efforts, her friends were being left behind through lack of effort. She said:

> Some people are quite happy to stuff sausages, that's how they like to live. A lot of my friends love to watch day-time TV, go out for a couple of hours, rave at the weekend. They don't want their heads in books. People might not think there is anything better for you, and you might be happy with the people that you've been with at the tomato packing factory and you don't want to leave. Mine was a personal choice and I want letters after my name cos no one in my family has done that.

A few women expressed the idea that the will to learn could lie dormant for years, and people had to wait for the right moment. Nadine (Iraqi/English, Art Foundation), who talked about her desperation at being an *'at home mum'* – said she had found the *'right moment'* to start her course, whilst for Tasha (black American/English, Access to Nursing) now was the *'right time'* because her children were older. Sherry (Guyanese/German, NVQ Classroom Assistant) said:

> It has to come from within ... It depends on personality and what they really want to do. It depends on where they are in their life, whether they want to do it, you know, it depends on whatever turning point they're going through.

Another prevalent view was that learning could not be forced. Nichole (three quarters Black/a quarter White, Basic Maths) said, *'Education is there if you want it – but you can't force people, it just depends on the person.'* According to Asha (Jamaican/Irish-English, B-Tech Beauty Therapy), parents were also superfluous in this respect: *'Some people are forced by their mums but if you're not interested you're not going to learn nuffink. Some people they just don't want to learn nuffink.'* Danielle (English/Jamaican, OCN Fashion and Clothing) flippantly remarked that nothing could make people want to learn, adding *'well, not unless you paid them'*, and laughed as she realised that her idea was probably not as disingenuous as it sounded.

Some respondents talked about the different attitudes to learning of teenage boys and girls. For Latesha (English/Jamaican, Certificate in Skills for Working Life), the predisposition towards learning was inherent and did not change as people, notably boys, got older. She asserted:

> Even with a second chance people would still mess up. I don't think it could change, it's just what the boys want, they're not willing to change theirselves. Girls, you can help them, but most girls are just like boys, you can't change them either.

Cassandra (Jamaican/Irish, Certificate in Skills for Working Life) said that young people messed up because of peer pressure not to study. This often resulted in bullying which was '*usually boys on boys and girls on girls*' and sometimes about race differences, but mostly about what people wore and whether '*it's in fashion or not, if you've got the new stuff.*' Cassandra said:

> Yeah, cos when you're young you don't think that it's really important to learn, and you get older you realise that you gotta learn, there's not really a choice ... Young people think that it's unpopular to go home and study, you should be out with your friends and getting into trouble, yeah, they think that's good, they might lose their reputation if they're studying their books a lot.

> Boys think college is pathetic, they're either smoking weed or making kids, 16 year-old boys or 15 get a girl pregnant, it's a sport to them, for them it's popular to chat about stuff like that, just tell them [the girls], 'do what you're doing about it', and they don't care, and that just messes up girls' lives ... they forget about the girls, it's just the next girl innit.

Cassandra's views support recent research which shows that boys' constructions of racialised and classed masculinities are linked to the ways in which they approach education. Constructions of 'bad boy' masculinities, in which boys present themselves as hard or cool, are made in opposition to education, and persist because they are a safe option in which their peer status is assured (Frosh *et al*, 2002; Archer and Yamashita, 2003b).

The students were asked how they thought the education system could be improved but the responses were too minimal to warrant a section in this book. Most of the women either responded that it could not be better, or felt that they had already addressed this question in their responses to other questions. Affirmative responses to this question were few. Jasmine (Grenadian-Scottish/Dominican) and Anabel (Guyanese/Indian-White) said that the role of the teacher in creating good working relations between students was important and should be improved. Jasmine talked about the problem of cultural separatism in her class – black people tended to stay on one side of the room and white people on the other – and how teachers should do much more to create a '*mixture of cultures in a class*'. She conceded that although making girls and boys work together had in her experience been successful in breaking down gender divisions, '*forcing cultures to mix might not work*'. Anabel also said that teachers were crucial in helping to alleviate black students' sense of inferiority, and believed that black students would be more motivated to learn if they felt equal to other students. She pointed out that teachers were afraid of '*getting involved for fear of losing their jobs*' over accusations of favouritism or race discrimination. This parallels the reluctance of some white college lecturers to comment on whether they had mixed race students in their classes. Ruby (Punjabi Indian/Irish) noted that not everyone was equally included in education and the impact this had on employment opportunities, adding '*even though people deny that – just look at who's employed in the universities – white middle-class*'. Ruby and Anisha (Indian/American) talked at length about internalised race and class barriers to learning. Their views are discussed in the next chapter.

Education: concluding remarks

Chapter Seven has shown how the women's talk around education reproduced the prevailing government and policy discourses on education. It is clear that a profound homogeneity of discourse exists. The policies present a vision of society as meritocratic, and that socio-economic background is ultimately irrelevant to a person's success. Individuals are constructed as autonomous and rational, capable of taking measures to free themselves from the shackles which have prevented them from being self-directed. They are the makers of their own destiny. The understanding is that any constraints on social mobility can be relatively easily overcome by the efforts of people themselves.

The vast majority of the women reflected the discourses of the inherent value of education, learning as an investment for material and personal reward, equality of opportunity and individual responsibility in their talk. Their communications also suggested that whilst they believed in meritocracy, their plans for the future may not translate into reality.

Many women also expressed the view that some people were less equal than others. However, articulations about their own and other people's educational chances suggested that the majority of women were unaware of, or chose not to talk about, the impact of structural constraints on the kinds of choices and decisions available. Being responsible individuals enabled people to make autonomous decisions within an egalitarian system of governance, and they were seen as ultimately responsible for their own success or failure (Beck and Beck-Gernsheim, 2001; Colley and Hodkinson, 2001). Two discourses were at work in the policies and the women's talk which are difficult to reconcile: the women reproduced the government's social inclusion discourse in that they believed that people's choices and chances could be impeded by poverty or disability, although they saw themselves as exempt from such constrictions, but they also drew on the discourses of equality of opportunity and self-responsibility in that it was up to the individual to take up the educational opportunities on offer.

Not only was personal success ultimately down to self-responsibility and self-motivation, but many of the women suggested that predisposition towards learning was innate, that it came from within. Inequalities were therefore explained in terms of an inherent lack within individuals themselves. Rather than understanding inequalities as big issues, they were reduced to small issues which the people themselves could, or could not – depending on predisposition – overcome. The onus of responsibility for society's ills and inequalities was not seen as the responsibility of government, but of the individuals themselves. This finding suggests that some of the women were close to claiming that people who are educationally disadvantaged through poverty and disability are themselves to blame. It is similar to how some of the women drew on race essentialist discourse in which different 'kinds' of people represent more or less desirable personality traits.

The ways in which the women talked about their everyday identities were fundamentally different from how they constructed their student identities. Whilst the issue of race was emphasised in articulations on identity, race and other traditional categories such as class and gender were underplayed in talk on education. This finding is underpinned by the post-feminist discourse, and supports a study by Volman and Ten Dam (1998) who found that students believed that gender differences should not have relevance, and refused to acknowledge them because inequality was seen as old-fashioned. Whilst most women said they experienced racial discrimination and marginalisation in their everyday lives, in the context of education they felt equal to others. The findings have considerable implications for a feminist political project which has mixed heritage women in mind: this is explored in Chapter Nine.

The vast majority of the women gave the impression that they had wholly bought into government discourses around education, and gave no indication that they were aware of the pernicious side-effects of these discourses. Only a small number of them were critical of government and education policy, and talked about race, class and gender inequalities in relation to education: this is the theme of the next chapter.

8

On race, class and gender

M ost of the women talked about their experiences of education and their opinions of education policy, but did not reflect on how discourses positioned them in society. This chapter focuses on what a few of them said about how they felt race and class impacted on people's choices and a sense of limitation. These respondents' views reflected those of education researchers who have argued that structural inequalities circumscribe the kinds of choices which are available to some people (Ball *et al*, 2000; Archer *et al*, 2003). However, despite these women's critical stance on government and education policy discourses, they were no less embroiled in the dominant discourse of individualism and related discourses than the other respondents.

Breaking the mould: '*The brains are not different, it's just something you've stamped on us*'

The New Labour government have stated that they aim to make school-leaving at the age of 16 a thing of the past. By 2010 the intention is for 50 per cent of people under 30 to be in higher education (Mizen, 2003, 259). Reay *et al* (2001) have pointed out that the decision to go to university, whilst routine for most middle-class people, is active and rationalised for people from working-class backgrounds. In a study of working-class people's participation in Higher Education, Archer *et al* (2002) found that their respondents believed that working-class people were more likely to experience disadvantages.

Eight women in my study planned to go to university. All would be the first in their families to do so. They all intended to go to new universities, reflecting the fact that a much higher proportion of people from ethnic minority backgrounds go to new rather than old universities (Tomlinson, 2001). Kerry (English/Bajan) and Kim (African [Cuban-Jamaican]/English) were breaking the mould in being the first in their families to study in further education, and to be going to university. In this sense, they were moving beyond the limitations of their social capital. Bourdieu's (1977) notions of *habitus*, and the idea that people internalise a sense of their own limits which constrain choice and action, do not correspond with the government rhetoric of freedom of choice, meritocracy and individual responsibility. The amalgamation of disposition, attitudes and practices which unconsciously dispose the person to act in particular ways occur in particular social contexts such as education. According to Bourdieu (1977), people are largely bound by their *habitus* and access to cultural or economic capital. For some this may be experienced as boundless possibility, whereas for others the *habitus* is limiting because they lack the required social capital to belong to the more privileged class.

Kerry's parents may have known their limits but Kerry also felt she knew hers, which were different from those of her parents. She had been discouraged from going to university by her family, but had nevertheless applied for and gained a place at Newcastle University to study performing arts. She said she '*couldn't see any other avenue to take*'. Initially her parents were not happy about this because of the financial burden, but they reached a solution. Kerry said:

> My dad was like – what're you going to do when you leave, it's a complete waste of time, you're going to be stuck back here, you won't get a job. But now they're more kind of proud cos I'll be the first one to go in the family and the first one that's wanted to go in the family, and they're being really supportive. If Dad hadn't saved for my wedding he wouldn't have had money to give me to go to university and I couldn't have gone. So I got university instead of a wedding!

Like Kelly, Kim pushed the limits in so far as she was the first in her family to go to university, but she knew her place when it came to the choice of university. Her place was influenced by entrenched class and race norms and the desire to protect herself in a society in which 'race underlies everything'. Kim was critical of what she saw as the distinction between élite and other universities because she felt it epitomised the scourge of race and class divisions within British society. However, according to Kim, working-class black, mixed race and ethnic minority people would not want to rupture the educational bastion of the middle and upper classes, even if they could. Kim seemed to talk about race and class interchangeably. Gender was not explicitly mentioned. This rather long quote allows the reader to engage with Kim's train of thought.

> Why would you want to put yourself in a racial environment for three years, no sensible person would put themselves somewhere where you could be at harm whether mentally or physically? ... Here [at the FE college she was attending] they said if anyone wanted to apply to Cambridge they said they could bring people from Cambridge in to talk about it, and everyone laughed 'that's for white people', and the black and Indian people all laughed. As far as we're concerned we're working-class people, always have been. Cambridge is a place where the Queen's children go, and the Queen is not associated with us! As far as she's concerned we are the people who pack her food, that's it! We wouldn't be able to mingle with people from that class because as far as they're concerned we are scum. Now to put yourself in an environment where you are considered the lowest of the low when you could be somewhere else, get a degree and have a nice time with it, meet people on your level, you're not going to put yourself there if you have any sense. A friend Yolanda got a first class degree at Stratford University, and got into UCL but she would not go there for the simple fact that that is not her level of people, as far as she's concerned even though she's got her degree she's not above none of us. I think that's the difference, the snobbery you would get from people who are classed as higher class than you or have always had money. So for us to get a degree is something special in a sense, to say, even though we've not been brought up like you the brains are not different, it's just something you've stamped on us cos you want to make yourself look bigger, it's just the status at the end of the day and that status is what causes the harm. Cos if you think you're better than someone else you automatically get nastiness.

If I got a place at Cambridge tomorrow I wouldn't go ... that's not my bag at all. If I'm going to go somewhere I want to know that I'm free to learn, that's it, I don't want the pressure of class being put on me, or my race, or people telling me I'm beneath them.

The education system don't like mixing people, they don't even like mixing what they consider normal people with disabled people, so why they going to mix classes? I think they like to keep people down, this country loves to think that they need people above other people to control the little people. The only time you come together is when you bump into each other in the street – they don't want people to be taught to grow up together and to accept each other.

Kim's views resonate with respondents in Archer *et al*'s (2002) study who saw access to better universities as the reserve of usually white middle-class students with the requisite resources and status. However, Kim reflected on how people were positioned in society by discourses and practices. She argued that the dominant culture transmitted to the marginal culture but not the other way round, and that as a black, mixed race and working-class person contestation of hegemony was extremely limited. However, she also defended her and her friend's decision not to go to an élite university from a position of agency, presenting this as an autonomous choice. This can be understood as a form of resistance against assimilation into what Kim saw as the white racist and classist institutions of higher education, in which attendance at an élite university would be a scourge rather than a blessing. Kim's views can be understood from the point of view that people are not simply passive players within dominant discourses, but still have limited choices (Reay and Ball, 1997).

Kim's comments are reminiscent of the working-class girls in McRobbie's (2000) study. These girls saw the middle-class girls in their school as educationally competitive and as snobs set apart by their accents and their parents' wealth, yet at the same time they enjoyed themselves and transcended the competition game, knowing that they were 'really brainy' anyway (McRobbie, 2000, 57). Kim's reflections also underscore the idea that it is incumbent upon individuals to see themselves as shaping their own lives, in which a person's life events are not attributed to external causes but to their own choices, abilities and capacities (Beck and Beck-Gernsheim, 2001, 25).

Assimilation and separatism: '*Choose to become educated ... but don't be friends with white people*'

Anisha (Indian/American) also talked about the impact of internalised race and class barriers on the educational opportunities people felt were available to them. The problem of educational inequalities in terms of access and participation could not be rectified by simply creating opportunities for black and mixed race students, because individuals settled into proscribed roles without being aware of it:

> I think it's the way you think about yourself – the way a lot of young black people grow up thinking that they have a particular set of opportunities that I think is smaller than the way white people are thinking. It's more than just low expectations, because it's not like you desire all those things and you just think, oh I'll never make it because I won't have the chances. I think there are people who don't even desire those things, because if you're not socialised into thinking that you will have this kind of education, you will do this, you will have these professional aspirations, you will go to university, I think it's a totally different way of thinking.

Anisha made a connection between internalised barriers to learning and assimilation. She said that the black people she knew had been socialised into believing that being educated was tantamount to capitulation to whiteness. Resistance to whiteness, and therefore to education, was the dominant discourse in education. In her opinion, the pressure for black and mixed race people to both assimilate and keep themselves separate from white people meant a constant search for the middle ground between these two positions. In the past, Anisha had had to negotiate and define her own position as a mixed race person in relation to the discourse of assimilation, and in relation to what she perceived as the prejudice of black people:

> It's the whole thing of giving in to a mainstream culture, you're making a point by not doing it, you reject all that stuff, cos maybe in part all that stuff rejected you and your people a long time ago, so why buy into that ... I find it strong among black friends I have and the peer pressure I get in terms of mixing with whites and doing what white people do. You can choose to become educated, but within that don't become part of the mainstream white culture, don't be friends with white people, have your own, and I know there was very much, from the other side, dis-

crimination, and it was all self-perpetuating – oh the blacks want to keep separate so we don't want anything to do with them, you know, all these things become a vicious circle.

The work of Robert Park (1952) is useful for understanding Anisha's perspective on assimilation. Park claimed that in the face of threat from minority groups, the dominant group would act to try and preserve its status through community cohesion. In response to the racial prejudice such conflict engendered, subordinate groups could either assimilate or take a separatist position: assimilation was more likely when the economy was strong, and separatism when it was weak. Anisha's views also support a study by Fordham (1988). In this study, black people who took on a raceless persona and assimilated into the white school culture were academically the most successful students; the other black students tried to juggle their allegiances to their school and their community, but in trying not to seem too white, sacrificed their cultural integrity. Anisha's and Kim's articulations suggest that some mixed heritage people face considerable tensions *vis-á-vis* education: they align themselves with the dominant group to achieve a certain status and acceptance, and simultaneously try to maintain a degree of cultural separatism and integrity.

A case of black and white: '*This equality thing has gone too far, personally...*'

Some of Nadine's (Iraqi/English) comments were controversial, and unapologetic articulations of what many people who are tired of the politically correct rhetoric around race, culture and immigration actually think. Nadine believed that everyone should live according to their own inclinations and be free to practice their customs, so long as they assimilated into mainstream culture. Nadine saw non-assimilation as wilful separatism, which was not in the interests of her children's education, nor of British society generally, and had resulted in the violation of the rights of the dominant host group. From Nadine's perspective, it seemed that the dominant group had failed to preserve its status and the minority group was now in control (Park, 1952).

According to Nadine, the government had over-stepped the mark in its commitment to equality, and been duped by people who had had everything offered to them but had deliberately kept themselves separate from mainstream British society. Unlike Kim and Anisha, who engaged with the complex and nuanced ways in which people were positioned by race discourses, Nadine saw the problem simplistically:

> People choose to live in this country and don't behave in a way that is beneficial to this country – like not learning the language, and I get irritated that my children can't understand their accent. I feel this equality thing has gone too far, personally. That sounds very racist doesn't it? I think everybody is entitled to believe in whatever culture, follow whatever culture they want, and have whatever religion, and it is wonderful that children are taught about different religions and different cultures and things. But what I do object to is where it impinges on other people's way of life. They segregate themselves within the society, they close themselves off, refuse to mix with the rest of society. It's a bit of a generalisation I know, I mean I met plenty that proved me wrong, but on the whole it is one of my real irritations, I suppose.

Nadine boldly insisted on 'political incorrectness'. She rejected cultural separatism because she saw it as the root cause of division within British society. Nadine believed that without race there would be no discrimination in the education system or the labour market. In the same way as an accent is a marker of difference and should be eradicated, race as a visible marker of difference should be eliminated. Nadine's position is open to the same criticism as that of advocates of equal opportunities policies: that they bypass the root causes of cultural separatism, and the real effects of constructions of race, gender and class on people's lives.

The women discussed in this chapter all believed that equal opportunities policies have failed, albeit for different reasons. Nadine's universalistic assimilatory stance raises the question of how we deal with difference in policy, practice and theory. Kim and Anisha spoke about internalised barriers, and how people are positioned in unfavourable ways by government discourses and practices around race, class and education. Kim's talk raises the crucial question of whether antiracist and anticlassist theories and policies are invalidated by discourses of individualisation and the praxis of individualised lifestyles. Anisha brings the debate full circle in raising the issue of how to deal with in-betweenness in terms of race and education. In the final chapter of this book, the themes of race, mixed race and education are brought together.

9

At the interface of discourse

In this final chapter, the main themes and discourses arising from the interviews are revisited and examined within the context of the broader discourses and theories around mixed heritage and further education. Part One focuses on the ways in which the discourses of postmodernism, essentialism and individualism were drawn upon and intersected in the women's constructions of identity. It especially highlights the ways in which the issue of race was a focal point in the women's talk. Part Two draws on the education data to discuss the dominance of the discourse of individualism and the dearth of race. Part Three returns to the theme of feminist politics introduced at the start of this book, and asks whether it has any practical application in relation to mixed heritage women in Britain today.

Part One: The interplay between postmodernism, essentialism and individualism

Contemporary postmodern/post-structuralist theories on identity, race, and mixed race accentuate the socially constructed, multiple, and fluid nature of identity. Recent post-compulsory education policies, on the other hand, refer to personhood largely in universalistic individualist terms, in which the person is an autonomous and self-responsible individual who is striving for completion. The two versions of personhood evident in the two sets of literature are not that dissimilar. In both sets of literature the surface overlay of the person may be culturally different, but the real person underneath is equal to all others.

In this study the discourses of essentialism, pluralism and individualism were mutually inclusive of each other rather than competing, and were drawn upon in a variety of interconnecting ways in the women's talk. This was a major finding and it showed that postmodern theory may overplay the fluid nature of identity and underplay the fixed dimension of identity. Furthermore, contrary to the view that individualised identities are fundamentally at odds with essentialist formations of selfhood, the women's talk revealed that the discourses of individualism and race essentialism sat comfortably together.

Postmodernism: limited versatility

The findings of this study adhere to the postmodern principles of multiplicity and fluidity in several ways. The women defined themselves as dual-racial, and in some cases as multiply-racial (see Tizard and Phoenix, 2001; Aspinall, 2003). Most women felt that people should have the freedom to define themselves, and that mixed race could encompass a wide range of identity combinations. Some respondents evoked a race equals culture equation in their expressions of cosmopolitan liberal ideas around mixed race, and used terms about race, culture, nationality and religion interchangeably. This notion that race equals culture reflects the tendency in public discourse to see the person as raceless: the concept of culture becomes the significant aspect of difference in place of race. This can be explained as a response to the view that cultural difference is harmless and enriching, whereas race is not (Frankenberg, 1993).

The women's descriptions of their friendships as wide-ranging and diverse also reflected this cosmopolitan discourse. Most women saw other people's curiosity about them as positive and some said that mixed race was a good thing because it made people more aware of difference. Yet few women actually saw their own difference as an asset. It is possible that these women constructed themselves as pedagogues and drew on the popular discourse which constructs mixed heritage people as bridge-builders between today's inequitable world and a better raceless future.

The women's conceptions of mixed race identity also echoed the postmodernist position in that they talked about adapting themselves to different situations and moving back and forth between, or merging, the two halves of themselves. However, contrary to the commonly held idea that mixed race identities epitomise the postmodern subject, most women did not talk about their identities as fundamentally dynamic, nor did they see themselves as amalgams of different race-free cultural selves. Whilst many of them advocated the idea of self-defining as mixed heritage in myriad ways, when they actually defined themselves as mixed race, they drew strongly on notions of fixed racial heritage and especially their parental heritages. They did not see themselves as free-floating entities in the postmodern sense, but communicated ideas around personhood within a spirit of limited versatility, in which fluid and static aspects of the person co-existed. The theme of essentialism warrants further discussion.

Essentialism: the significance of race

Most respondents made sense of their lives through the lens of race: for many, race was not an unpalatable or unnameable aspect of life, as much social science literature and public discourse suggests, but was a significant aspect of their identity and self-understanding, and intrinsic to their experiences of categorisation, exclusion and discrimination. The dominance of race in the women's talk challenges sociological and feminist literature on identity, and the current popular view of identity which draws on postmodern and multicultural discourse and mini-mises the significance of race. Structuralist theories are usefully applied to raced ways of thinking around identity which concern a notion of selfhood which is not variable or subject to change. Modernist feminist theory, too, relies on an essential subject as the basis for a feminist re-form project.

Race was a trenchant aspect of the women's lives. Almost half the sample stated emphatically that race and colour were not important in how they defined themselves, thus dismissing formal classifications based on external racial markers of identity. Many also saw being mixed race as an important aspect of their identities. Race was a powerful theme in their talk on friendships, feelings of difference, categorisation, exclusion and discrimination. Whilst destabilising one race essentialist discourse in their rejection of homogeneous constructions of race, they simultaneously upheld other race essentialist discourses in their constructions of identity. Thus they constructed ideas around race in paradoxical ways: on the one hand, they rejected race, and on the other, they utilised it. However, these positions were not actually contradictory. Race as a means of self-definition, as opposed to race as a means of categorisation, seemed to be a powerful aspect of identity precisely because of the denial of their mixed race identity, and their experiences of mis-categorisation and discrimination. It may have been an act of defiance or resistance against being wrongly categorised, and against the mono-heritage norm: I am me, I am mixed race. It may have been an expression of the right to be different, and an assertion of difference as positive and worthy of celebration.

The data support the traditional, and many would say outdated, view that mixed race people are black. Almost all the women in the study felt that they were wrongly perceived and categorised by others in mono-heritage terms; some were seen as black or Asian, a few as white, and some as possessing a heritage totally unconnected to either one of their parental heritages. Tasha, who was black American/English, said she was often seen as Chinese, and Frida, who was Colombian/Polish Jewish-English, said people usually thought she was Indian or Pakistani. This suggests that, despite the prevalence of mixed heritage people, and postmodern and multicultural ways of thinking about identity, there is still an assumption that people are mono-racial.

In asserting their mixed raceness, some women defined themselves in relation to homogeneously perceived others. They did this by drawing on essentialist notions of blackness and whiteness, in which distinctive attitudes and ways of behaving were linked to a person's race. Constructions of mixed race were sometimes made in opposition to black identity. This could be seen in communications around friendship and experiences of discrimination, and was implicit in some of the women's talk about education.

Race was also a dominant feature in that self-identification as mixed race was expressed by many women as an assertion of the racial heritages of both parents, where this heritage was understood as literally constituting the women's identities. Respondents were precise about their exact racial mix, traced back to parents and often grandparents, even where the father was absent or marginal, and regardless of whether the respondent was brought up in a white or black household.

Parental heritage was also emphasised in the women's talk about their identity evolution, which involved an initial denial or rejection, and the subsequent embracing, of their mixed race identity.

The findings showed that racial discrimination was flagrant. Several women of African or Caribbean/white origin felt that they had been incorrectly categorised as black, and believed they were not seen as white enough by white people nor as black enough by black people. Whilst it has been recognised that mixed heritage people experience racism from white people (Parker and Song, 2001; Tizard and Phoenix, 2001; Ali, 2003) there has been virtual silence on the subject of discrimination from black people, although it was acknowledged in a recent UK study on mixed heritage children (DfES, 2004). This may be due in part to the established view that mixed race people are black, and that therefore any discrimination against them by black people is not acknowledged as racial discrimination. The question here is whether a politically motivated mixed heritage movement is needed to counter discrimination which is specific to mixed heritage people.

The theory of postmodernism is difficult to sustain because of the many ways in which the women talked about the dominance of race in their lives. Most of them categorically rejected racial designations, and simultaneously felt they were perceived by others in racially designated ways (see Zack, 1995). It is possible that the discourse of homogeneity, and experiences of exclusion and misnaming, contributed to the women's refusal to endorse categorisation, and simultaneously gave them the feeling that they could assert their own heterogeneous mixed race identities which were not understood in categorical terms. Yet they drew on race discourse to define themselves: these self-identifications usually endorsed parents' racial heritages, and were sometimes invoked in opposition to racially homogeneous others such as black people. The danger here is that some mixed heritage people may fall into the same exclusionist trap as advocates of race homogeneity. This recourse to essentialist discourse has recently been facilitated by new discourses around race biology and the ever-increasing fascination with the supposed link between DNA testing and notions of 'who we really are' (Skinner, 2004).

The dominant discourse of individualism, and how this connected with the discourses of postmodernism and essentialism in the women's talk about identity, is discussed next.

Individualism: mixed race as an aspect of personality

Many respondents had no conceptual difficulty in isolating self-definition as mixed race from the idea of race as a category and a form of social ascription. In describing what was significant in their self-definitions of personhood, many women said that their personalities were important, and most also said that being mixed race was important. An easy alignment was made between being mixed race and personality: the women felt they were unique individuals, and being mixed race was an intrinsic part of that.

In talking about appearance, the women usually focused on hair and skin colour yet were anxious to explain that their identities were not based on the superficial designations of race or colour, but on who they were beneath their skin. They made a distinction between exterior and interior facets of identity, separating the spurious markers of race, which related to appearance and categorisation, from a primary sense of the self, which was about individual personality. This shows how individualist and postmodernist discourses of personhood are similar: the core unique aspect of the individual lies beneath the aspect of selfhood which may be culturally different. The unique self, expressed in the assertion 'I am just me, I am mixed race', also utilises essentialist discourse in that it draws on the idea of fixed racial heritage.

So what conclusions can be drawn from Part One *apropos* the existing literature? Essentialist theory is not given much credence in the social science literature on race or ethnic identity, and postmodernist and post-structuralist theories predominate. This research, however, suggests that postmodernist theories of identity cannot be wholly endorsed. The findings on identity to some extent reflect the post-structuralist notion that the self is socially constituted, and also correspond with post-structuralist theory in so far as many women felt their identities were determined by other people's positioning, and that identities were fluid and subject to change (Butler, 1990, 1993). The findings are also consistent with a humanist position, and resonate with the theory of biological foundationalism in that the women drew on fixed race essentialist notions of selfhood, and race was a trenchant aspect of their lives (see Bordo, 1989). Traditional mono-heritage essentialist theory is also challenged by the findings, and it seems that a model of dual or multiple essentialisms may be more appropriate for contextualising mixed heritage identities. Root's (1992) notion of mixed race identities which are multiple and socially ambiguous, and contained within typified racial boundaries, is useful for understanding this twin position.

In keeping with the social constructionist approach, the discourses drawn upon by the women were not mutually exclusive but overlapped: the self was understood as uniquely individual, constructed and versatile, and bounded by fixed racial categories. The discourses of postmodernism, essentialism and individualism were therefore mutually inclusive, but ultimately the discourse of individualism prevailed and subsumed the other two. This can be seen in the following ways.

The women drew on postmodern discourse in their articulations around the multiplicity and fluidity of identities. In so doing they reproduced a discourse of postmodern particularism, in which identities and categories are broken down into smaller and smaller parts and become progressively specific and individualised. This is seen not only in the ways in which the women described mixed race in anything goes terms, but also in how multiple heritages were drawn upon in their constructions of selfhood. Cerisse, for example, described herself as Scottish-African/Zambian-English, Jennifer as Caribbean-Portuguese-Asian/English-Irish, and Lekeisha as 'fully mixed' Jamaican-Indian-Chinese-Turkish. As far as society was concerned, these women could simply have defined themselves as black.

Thus postmodern particularism is a discourse of individualism. It opposes essentialism in that it challenges the idea of identities or categories based on fixed, consistent and shared homogenous characteristics. But it is also an essentialist discourse, as it utilises discrete race categories, albeit many of them at the same time. So in constructing themselves as unique mixed race individuals, the women drew on all three discourses simultaneously.

Part Two: Education, individualism, and the irrelevance of race

The women's position on race was an ambivalent one. Within the broader context of everyday experience the theme of race was salient. Reflections on education, however, focused robustly on the government discourses of equity and individual responsibility, and explicit articulations around race were dropped altogether. Part Two explores this ambiguity around race, and highlights the paradox, as articulated by Goldberg (1993): race is irrelevant but all is race.

Education, education, education: a homogeneity of discourse

The findings in the two chapters on education revealed that there was remarkable uniformity between the women's views and opinions on education, and the wider government and policy discourses around education and personhood. The umbrella discourses of economic competitiveness and social justice, and the associated discourses of the value of education, equality of opportunity and individual responsibility, permeated the policy discourses of learning as an investment for economic and personal reward, the individual's responsibility to learn, and the idea that individuals have agency and the power to effect positive change in society.

The women reproduced the government and policy discourses in talk about their own experiences and beliefs about education. People were constructed as rational and autonomous, operating within an egalitarian system of governance. Those who remained uneducated had made that choice, or were not predisposed towards learning, and only had themselves to blame for their lack of education. The women therefore discounted the structural mechanisms and failure of resources through which social inequality was generated, and suggested that inequalities were not seen as the responsibility of government but of people themselves. Any criticisms they made of government policy focused on particular elements or effects of discourses, rather than the discourses themselves.

The findings are testimony to the success of neo-liberalism. They illustrate the power of neo-liberal discourses to locate responsibility in the individual, and pathologise any underachievement as personal failure (see Bauman, 2005). The mass availability of education may have been seen as a marker of an equal society; certainly most women indicated that their own educational achievements were testimonies to the success of government policies and initiatives which aimed to provide greater equality of opportunity in education. Education was seen as the panacea for all ills, a great equaliser of difference which could iron out any inequalities.

Authoritarianism has disappeared in the neo-liberal language of freedom of choice and equality of opportunity which makes it so easy, and even incumbent on the person, to buy into current discourses around education. Most women were not consciously aware of how they were positioned by the discourse of individualism, but this is not surprising. Discourses become imbued within the subject, and the individualised subject becomes the object of education. Within a culture of responsibility to the self, choices around education are made within the framework of education as a right and a self-duty: the do or die scenario, in which those who do can never do enough, and those who do not become what Fergusson *et al* (2000) has referred to as 'status zero' (p289). Dominant discourses become part of personal narratives which support and uphold these discourses. It is only through this process of reproduction that people feel that they have control over their lives.

The irrelevance of race

The individual within the context of education was understood by the women as capable of making rational, instrumentalist choices within a structural vacuum; any inequalities were inextricably linked to the actions and personalities of individuals themselves, rather than to external factors which impinged on people's educational choices and achievements. Therefore, whilst there was interplay between pluralist, essentialist and individualist discourses in the women's constructions of selfhood, they invariably reflected the discourse of individualism in their talk about education. In this discourse of individualism, race was rarely referred to in the context of education, and not perceived as a marker of disadvantage. This stands in stark contrast to how race was talked about in relation to the women's daily experiences, as discussed in Part One.

The women's talk was underpinned by education models of inclusion which have largely assumed that racial and cultural difference are no longer relevant to how we understand policy and practice (Gillborn, 1996). The perceived irrelevance of race within the context of education is symptomatic of 'colour-blindness' to the reality of race (Ahmed, 1997; Tessman, 1999). It reflects a discourse of whiteness in which, as Phoenix (1997) has pointed out, the person is understood as raceless. This notion of racelessness is propped up by the postmodernist discourse of identity, and the celebratory discourse of mixed heritage, in which personhood is constructed in benign cultural terms and race deemed invisible. The idea of racelessness is also underpinned by individualist discourse, which translates into universalistic ways of constructing personhood. In recent post-compulsory education policy, for example, particular identities and categories have been subsumed within universal meta-categories such as 'under-represented people' and 'the disadvantaged' (DfEE, 1999).

As the focus is increasingly deflected away from race within education policy and popular multiculturalist discourse, racial power dynamics also disappear. Certainly the education findings have suggested that race and race inequality are not big issues for the women in the study. However, if race is trivialised, racism is seen as insignificant: it becomes de-institutionalised, and people are rendered free from the effects of differentiation and discrimination. If we juxtapose this absence of race with the individualist discourse of self-responsibility, it seems that *any* differences between people and the inequalities these engender are too readily redirected back onto the person, rather than being attributed to the effects of dominant/subordinate power relationships.

Many respondents felt that they were different from others, and encountered categorisation and discrimination in their daily lives. This problem was not defined in terms of how unequal power relations and hierarchical structures positioned them within racialised discourse, but in terms of personality and behaviour, and how individuals treated each other. Many respondents probably saw not only underachievement in education but also personal experiences of discrimination as the responsibility of individuals. Discrimination was therefore seen as a normal aspect of everyday life, and a problem for the individual to solve.

Part Three: A question of political strategy
Defining a mixed race identity: a newer community?

As discussed in Chapter Two, the modernist/postmodernist debate within western feminist philosophy has been paralleled by a similar debate in black feminism which has focused on the need to uphold race as a social category, as opposed to womanhood, for effective political action. A modernist black feminist perspective demands a mixed race category or a black category which incorporates mixed race experiences for countering categorisation and discrimination, and for working towards greater racial equality. This position has been criticised for being a universalistic conception which inevitably results in exclusion and derision (Anthias and Yuval-Davis, 1992; Brah, 1994). The findings in this study support this criticism: derision and exclusion were cited by many respondents as intrinsic to their everyday experiences of perceived difference, categorisation and discrimination, such as the experience of not being black enough.

Several researchers in the US and the UK have claimed that there is a desire for a mixed race category, and have grappled with the problem of finding a model of personhood which includes mixed heritage women's experiences (Ifekwunigwe, 1999; Mahtani and Moreno, 2001; Olumide, 2002; Rockquemore and Brunsma, 2002). Ifekwunigwe (2001) has argued that the challenge for mixed race theory and identity is how to construct an inclusive space for mixed race people which does not resort to essentialist categories, nor to a solely individualist concept of selfhood, and which is simultaneously a space which allows for alliances to arise because of shared marginal status (p45).

The theories put forward by these authors attempt, laudably, to incorporate the diversity of mixed race experiences into a concept of personhood which may form the basis for a common politics. However, they would be difficult to translate into practice for the women in this study. Not one of them expressed a desire for a political or a social category of mixed race, and few indicated that they wanted any kind of political or social reform.

Although they had no wish to belong to a category of mixed race, mixed race was a profoundly meaningful identity for the women. Asserting mixed race identity meant forging a unique individuality. But it may have been premised on a recognition of shared experience, or an 'imagined community' in which the women felt united with other mixed race people (Anderson, 1983). It can also be understood in terms of Bourdieu's (1984) notion of distinction, involving a process which unites those whose heritage is mixed, and distinguishes them from all others (p56). In Ali's (2003) study, the children's family histories were evoked to create links with imagined places and people to make sense of their racial identity. Similarly, some of the women in my study drew on ideas around their own often marginalised racial and cultural heritages to construct their identity. Having a sense of their own origins and their relatedness to other mixed heritage people may therefore have been more important than identifying with or belonging to a specific group or category.

The notion of solidarity and collective action across categorical boundaries is far more useful than focusing on a fixed mixed race category. In the last two decades, social theorists have attempted to go beyond the modernist/postmodernist *impasse* by shifting the spotlight away from the essentialist body to political sites of struggle which focus on common causes, and foregrounding the ways in which personhood is constructed through social and political relations and practices (Mouffe, 1995; Nicholson and Seidman, 1995; Ashenden, 1997). The question of politics, and whether collective political formations are possible in the present climate of the depoliticised subject, is discussed in the final two sections of this book.

Individualism and the de-politicised subject

The vast majority of the women saw themselves as outside the realm of politics *per se*. Whilst some individual respondents may have regarded themselves as political, neither politics, nor a collective identity which rallied around the concerns and interests of mixed heritage women, were pressing issues for any of the women. Given the current individualistic and post-feminist climate, these findings are not at all surprising. The data supports the view that feminism has a normalised and legitimised popular version, in which women enjoy greater freedoms than ever before, and a political version which is virtually redundant in the post-feminist climate of today (McRobbie, 2000). The women's lack of politicisation was most clearly shown in the assertion that any inequalities which did exist were the problem and responsibility of individuals themselves, rather than a problem of structure and resources which should be solved by government. Responsibility was clearly about the self and not the collective other. Race discrimination was also a normal part of everyday life, and the responsibility for overcoming discrimination on the individual herself.

Only one respondent identified as politically black, and nobody explicitly referred to their own mixed race identity as a political identity. Ruby said being politically black was linked to her experiences of racialisation, and involved a conscious resistance against these experiences. She also spoke of a newer community based on affiliation through shared marginal status (see Omi and Winant, 1994; Mouffe, 1995). The *'different place'* and *'next stage'* Ruby talked about was a space in which race was not an issue. She said:

> Being politically black – a lot of mixed race people will not claim that as an identity because they've moved on, they're in a different place from me – and I still am at that place because to me the most distressing experiences of my life have been in the way that I have been rejected because of the colour of my skin. And being able to use that, being able to claim that identity has enabled me to have a voice and explain what it felt like and the effect it's had on me and to know that people aren't going to say oh you're white really and you've just got a chip on your shoulder. Sometimes I feel I'm ready to move on to the next stage but there's a bit of confusion because I am also Irish, and that isn't included when I take the position of a black person, and I get quite concerned about that – I haven't worked that out and I feel that's the next step.

The challenge of mixed race studies is how to integrate the experiences of mixed heritage people into a comprehensible framework of personhood which recognises their experiences as racialised, individual and dynamic. My findings have shown that searching for ways to establish a mixed race category, as some other researchers have tried to do, is not a useful quest: the findings suggest that although there was a strong sense of mixed race as a unique identity, there was no interest in a category of mixed race.

Mixed race as a discourse and an identity were welcomed, but the political aspects of race, class and gender were seldom mentioned. There was nothing identity-specific about the needs of mixed race women in further education. Gender and the fact of being a woman were seldom mentioned by any of the respondents, and none of them identified as feminists. This corresponds with the assertion that few young women today identify as feminists, and feminist politics is seen as a waste of time (Whelelan, 1995). A feminist project with the interests of mixed heritage women and their education in mind would therefore seem to be redundant.

However, discriminatory attitudes and practices directed towards the women, as well as the ways in which they drew on race in their con- structions of identity, indicates an unequivocal need to investigate further the meaning of race within social discourse and in people's lives. It is clear that despite the lack of engagement in the political aspects of everyday life and education, some form of political intervention is needed to oppose the injustices experienced by mixed heritage people. This goes back to the questions posed at the beginning of this book: what form can political intervention take when people are politically disengaged, when they reproduce discourses and are unaware of how they are positioned by discourse?

Conclusion: engaging creatively with discourse

This book seeks to investigate mixed heritage women's constructions of identity and further education and to explore ways in which their ex- periences can create new knowledge and move education policy and feminist practice forward.

Hegemonic and less dominant discourses around race, mixed race and education were reproduced in the women's talk. The limitations of dis- course analysis have been patent. Analysing discourse reveals its circu- larity: discourse informs our knowledge and how we understand and speak about our experiences, and our experiences are spoken through discourse. The omnipresence of the discourse of individualism in this study is significant. This hegemonic discourse speaks against the possi- bility of collective engagement in politics because power relations are created within individualist discourses which prevent the development of the political subject. This inevitably has considerable implications for a feminist emancipatory politics: where people do not feel implicated in power relations and regard themselves as innocent by-standers, the possibility for emancipatory action is limited.

It is hard to see a way out of this politically de-motivated situation but it is important to try and find ways to overcome indifference. The discourse analytical approach has enabled us to see how aspects of the mixed heritage women's subjectivities and experiences were discursively produced and located in how they understood their own social position and racial identity. It has revealed the assumptions behind discourse, and how mixed heritage identities have been produced through discourses which support unequal power relations. It has also shown how the discourse of individualism gave the women an exaggerated sense of individual agency and control over their lives. However, although they were not critical of normative discourses in their conversations with me, this does not mean that the women were unaware of, and did not critically engage with the workings of discourse.

Critical pedagogy provides us with a way out of the limitations of discourse. In recognising and critiquing the ways in which the women are positioned by discourses, it is possible to develop an understanding of how these discourses place them in intricate and uneven power relationships and systems of domination, and how different experiences are constructed and legitimised. This is the first step to emancipation from these discourses.

Critical pedagogy also allows the creation of oppositional discourses. As Foucault has pointed out, discourse is never a complete thing, but involves overlapping, contingent and contradictory discourses. It is impossible to capture or control discourse because there is always some part of it that escapes which can form the basis of an alternative discourse: this is borne out of the dominant discourse, which may then serve to subvert the dominant discourse. Here lies the potential for change. Critical pedagogy involves harnessing the discontented part that has seeped out of the dominant discourse and using it to cultivate greater awareness in individuals which may help to build communities of resistance. Within the structured environment of the classroom and lecture theatre, one challenge is to engage with how people's experiences are constructed in terms of their historical, social and political locations. When they spoke about their experiences of difference, mis-categorisation and discrimination, the women in this study were talking politics, but without a collective voice. Mohanty (2003) puts it thus:

> The issue of subjectivity and voice thus concerns the effort to understand our specific locations in the educational process and in the institutions through which we are constituted. Resistance lies in self-conscious engagement with dominant, normative discourses and representations and in the active creation of oppositional analytic and cultural spaces. Resistance that is random and isolated is clearly not as effective as that which is mobilized through systematic politicized practices of teaching and learning. (p196)

Many educationalists and social theorists are already involved in the kind of work Mohanty proposes within their own disciplinary spheres. But the aim must be to normalise critical debate and activity within educational contexts, and ultimately within the public realm. This involves changing the meaning of democratic education: instead of producing market individuals, it should become a space for debating existing epistemologies such as capitalism, for contesting how knowledge is produced and legitimised, and for actively constructing something which can take its place.

This is certainly a critical moment of depoliticisation, a moment of empty postmodern diversity, empty constructions of selfhood, and a profound dearth in collective relationships and forms of action. But it is a perfect empty moment for the alternative discourse to flourish.

The advent of mixed heritage identity opens up the potential for new racially-based movements and, as Omi and Winant (1994) have argued, the 'creation of new identities, new racial meanings, and a new collective subjectivity' (p90). Feelings of difference, mis-categorisation and discrimination were experienced by the majority of women in the study: this was their common ground. In talking about these experiences they were talking about political issues. The most explicit political aspect of their talk was the distinction they made between these experiences and a more promising future in which the negative effects of race did not exist, where the very presence of mixed race people and their mediatory role as pedagogues would contribute to overcoming prejudices and inequities in society.

Whether emancipatory politics rally around an essentialist body or a common cause, feminism's commitment to the principle of justice is underpinned by the idea that individuals must organise collectively for political action to be effective. This political organisation does not need a mixed race essentialist subject, but it does require a political subject. The energy, inspiration and motivation felt by each individual needs to be collectively focused to make workable connections between anti-racist feminist thought and organised political activity. The era of the grand feminist project has passed, and people are trying to find different, smaller scale ways to challenge social, economic and educational injustice. In order for people to build communities of opposition to dominant discourses of oppression, they must engage critically with the ways in which discourses position people, and how reproducing these discourses normalises inequality and domination. Only through a critical approach to discourse, and the identification of assumptions around race essentialism, the celebration of postmodern diversity and individualism – which all have pernicious effects – can such discourses be subverted. Only then can subjugated knowledges determine alternative discourses which might lead to progressive change. We need to develop awareness of how women and men, black and white and mixed heritage people, are all implicated in intricate power relations. We need to understand our individualised states and find collective ways out of our isolation.

Appendix 1:
Profile of the women

Name	Age	Racial Self-designation	Course studied	Occupation/Children
Adriana	22	Angolan-Portuguese/Angolan (MF/SG)	Access to HE Law	
Anabel	40	Guyanese/Indian-White (MH)	Computer course (PT)	Teacher; Two children
Anisha	31	Indian/American (MF)	Ex-FE	Development Worker
Anita	16	Mauritian/Filipino (MF)	AS-Levels Government and Politics, Law, English	
Asha	16	Jamaican/Irish-English (M)	B-Tech Beauty Therapy	Youth Worker (PT)
Brenda	42	Afro-Caribbean/ Indian-white Jewish (MH)	Secretarial course (Ex-FE)	Secretary; Two children
Cassandra	16	Jamaican/Irish (M)	Certificate in Skills for Working Life	
Cerisse	16	Scottish-African/Zambian-English (M/MH)	Summer course – preparation for GCSEs	
Chantel	18	English/African (M)	ABC Adv. Business Studies	
Charmaine	16	Jamaican/White (MF)	NVQ Beauty Therapy	
Corinna	21	Jamaican/Irish (M)	NVQ Beauty Therapy	Sales Assistant (PT)
Danielle	17	English/Jamaican (M)	OCN Fashion and Clothing	
Dianne	17	Welsh/Mauritian (M)	A-Levels Law, Media, Psychology	Sales Assistant (PT)
Ella	16	Burmese/Mauritian (M)	A-Levels Psychology, Biology, Business, Media	Job in retail shop (PT)

Name	Age	Racial Self-designation	Course studied	Occupation/Children
Emma	16	Jamaican/English (M)	GNVQ Art & Design	One child (SP)
Frida	30	Columbian/Polish Jewish-English (M)	A-Levels Politics, History, English Lit.	One child (SP)
Jasmine	19	Grenadian-Scottish/ Dominican (M/SG)	GCSE Humanities	
Jennifer	17	Caribbean-Portuguese-Asian/ English-Irish (MF)	NVQ Beauty Therapy	Private clients (PT)
Keira	16	Nigerian/Filipino (MF)	AS-Levels Government and Politics, Law, History	
Kerry	21	English/ Bajan (MF)	B-Tech Performing Arts	Sales Assistant (PT)
Kim	21	African [Cuban-Jamaican]/English (M)	Access to HE Psychology	One child
Latesha	16	English/Jamaican (M)	Certificate in Skills for Working Life	
Lekeisha	17	'Fully mixed' Jamaican [Indian-Chinese-Turkish] (MH)	NVQ Hairdressing	Job in hairdressing salon (PT)
Lianne	21	St. Lucian/English (M)	NVQ Catering	MacDonalds Manager
Lesley	17	Bajan/Scottish (M)	NVQ New Directions	
Nadine	38	Iraqi/English (M)	Art Foundation (PT)	Cleaner; Pub worker; Two children

Name	Age	Racial Self-designation	Course studied	Occupation/Children
Nalia	22	Three quarters Black/a quarter Chinese (SG)	NVQ Administration	One child
Nichole	32	3/4 Black/ 1/4 White (SG)	Basic Maths	Nursery Nurse
Olga	25	Italian/Eritrean (M)	EFL	One child (SP)
Paula	16	Romanian/Greek	Diploma Public Services	
Peta	37	African/West Indian-English (MF/MH)	NVQ Childcare (Ex-FE)	Social Worker; Two children
Petra	17	African/Portuguese (MF)	GNVQ Foundation Science	
Rosa	33	Angolan-Portuguese/Portuguese (MF/SG)	B-Tech Hairdressing (PT)	Work with disabled children (PT)
Ruby	44	Punjabi Indian/Irish (adopted by white parents)	Legal Executive Certificate (Ex-FE)	Mental Health Worker; Writer
Sherry	31	Guyanese/German (F)	NVQ Classroom Assistant (PT)	Teaching Assistant; Three children (SP)
Siham	19	Eritrean/Egyptian (M)	GNVQ Business Studies	Work in shop
Soraya	38	English/Turkish (MF)	Basic Maths and English	Four children
Sumaira	22	Pakistani/English (F)	GCSE re-takes	Two children
Tania	39	West Indian/English (M)	B-Tech in Support; Foundation in Counselling Skills (Ex-FE)	Learning Support Assistant; Two children
Tasha	26	black American/English	Access to Nursing (PT)	Two children

The racial self-designations show the respondent's father's heritage first and her mother's heritage second. For example, 'Indian/English' would indicate that the respondent had an Indian father and an English mother.

Abbreviations and notes:

SG –   Second generation mixed race respondent (respondent had two heritages and one birth parent was mixed race).

MH –   Multiple heritage respondent (respondents had more than two heritages and neither parent was white).

M –   Respondent grew up, or mainly grew up, with birth mother.

F –   Respondent grew up, or mainly grew up, with birth father.

MF –   Respondent grew up, or mainly grew up, with both birth parents.

PT –   Part-time (courses and occupations were full-time unless stipulated otherwise).

SP –   Respondent is a single parent.

Ex-FE – Respondent was no longer enrolled on an FE course, but had been an FE student in the last 5 years.

Appendix 2:
Interview questions

Introductory questions

a) Name, age, self-description of 'mixed-ness'

b) autobiographical background: who brought up with, whether in mixed or mono-racial household, and which type of environment (gender/ethnic/class) brought up and schooled in

c) course studied, whether full or part-time, academic or vocational

d) occupation, children/dependants, disability

Identity

1. What is important to you in how you define who you are?

2. Do you feel that your sense of self has changed over time or due to some turning point in your life?

3. Are you drawn to particular groups of people – who are your friends?

4. Do you feel that you adapt in, or to, different cultural situations?

5. How do you think people you don't know see you? Does that influence the way you see yourself?

6. Do you feel different, or have you ever felt different to other people?

7. Are acquaintances and friends curious about your background?

8. What does the term mixed race mean to you? How do you feel about this term?

9. Have you ever experienced discrimination?

Education

11. Why did you choose this college and the course you are doing?

12. What have the positive aspects of the course been?

13. Have you experienced any problems with the course?

14. How do you see your future?

15. Do you feel you will have the skills and qualifications to be able to do that/get there?

16. What does a good education mean to you?

17. Do you feel you have had the same chances as everyone else in getting the education you want?

18. In its further education policy the government talks about being inclusive of all people. Do you think that everyone is equally included in education?

19. The government also talks about creating a 'culture of learning'. Do you think people can learn to want to learn?

20. Do you think the education system could be better?

Bibliography

Ahmed, S. (1997) 'It's a sun-tan, isn't it?': autobiography as an identificatory practice. In H. Mirza (ed) *Black British Feminism: a reader.* London: Routledge

Ainley, P. (1994) *Degrees of Difference: Higher Education in the 1990s.* London: Lawrence and Wishart

Ali, S. (2003) *Mixed-Race, Post-Race: gender, new ethnicities and cultural practices.* London: Berg

Alibhai-Brown, Y. (2001) *Mixed Feelings: the complex lives of mixed-race Britons.* London: Women's Press

Anderson, B. (1983) *Imagined Communities: reflections on the origin and spread of nationalism.* London: Verso

Anthias, F. and Yuval-Davis, N. (1992) *Racialised Boundaries: race, nation, gender, colour and class and the anti-racist struggle.* London: Routledge

Anzaldua, G. (1987) *Borderlands/La Frontera: the new mestiza.* San Francisco, California: Aunt Lute Books

Apple, M. (1999) The absent presence of race in educational reform. *Race, Education and Ethnicity*, 2(1): 9-16

Archer, L., Leathwood, C. and Hutchings, M. (working paper) (2002) HE: a risky business. In A. Hayton and A. Paczuska (eds) *Widening Access to Higher Education.* London: Kogan Page

Archer, L., Ross, A. and Hutchings, M. (2003) *Higher Education and Social Class: issues of inclusion and exclusion.* London: Routledge Falmer

Archer, L. and Yamashita, H. (2003a) 'Knowing their limits?' identities, inequalities and inner city school leavers' post-16 aspirations. *Journal of Education Policy*, 18(1): 53-69

Archer, L. and Yamashita, H. (2003b) Theorising inner city masculinities: 'race', class, gender and education. *Gender and Education*, 15(2): 115-132

Arnot, M., David, M., Weiner, G. (1999) *Closing the Gender Gap: post-war education and social change.* Cambridge: Polity Press

Asad, T. (1993) Multiculturalism and British identity in the wake of the Rushdie Affair. In T. Asad (ed) *Genealogies of Religion.* Baltimore: Johns Hopkins University Press

Ashenden, S. (1997) Feminism, postmodernism and the sociology of gender. In D. Owen (ed) *Sociology After Postmodernism*. London: Sage

Aspinall. P. (2003) The conceptualisation and categorisation of mixed race/ethnicity in Britain and North America: identity options and the role of the state. *International Journal of Intercultural Relations*, 27(3): 269-296

Aspinall, P. (2004) Seminar paper: Mixed: what the census can tell us, Institute of Education, University of London, June 2004

Assiter, A. (1996) *Enlightened Women: modernist feminism in a postmodern age*. London: Routledge

Avis, J., Bloomer, M., Esland, G., Gleeson, D. and Hodkinson, P. (1996) (eds) *Knowledge and Nationhood: education, politics and work*. London: Cassell

Back, L. (1994) *New Ethnicities and Urban Culture: racism and multiculture in young people's lives*. London: UCL Press

Bagley, C. and Young, L. (1979) The identity, adjustment, and achievement of transracially adopted children: a review and empirical report. In G. K. Verma and C. Bagley (eds) *Race, Education and Identity*. London: Macmillan Press

Ball, S. J. (1993) Self-doubt and soft data: social and technical trajectories in ethnographic fieldwork. In M. Hammersley (ed) *Educational Research: current issues*. Milton Keynes: Open University Press

Ball, S. J. (1994) *Education Reform: a critical post-structural approach*. Buckingham: Open University Press

Ball, S. J. (2000 [1993]) What is policy? Texts, trajectories and toolboxes. In S. J. Ball (ed) *Sociology of Education: major themes,* Vol. IV: 1830-1840. London: Routledge

Ball, S. J., Maguire, M. and Macrae, M. (2000) *Choice, Pathways and Transitions Post-16: new youth, new economies in the global city*. London: Routledge Falmer

Banks, N. (2002) Mixed race children and families. In K. N. Dwivedi (ed) *Meeting the Needs of Ethnic Minority Children Including Refugee, Black and Mixed Parentage Children: a handbook for professionals*. London: Jessica Kingsley Publishers

Bauman, Z. (2005) *Work Consumerism and the New Poor* (2nd Edition). Buckingham: Open University Press

BBC Website (news.bbc.co.uk/hi/English/static/in_depth/uk/2002/race/Changing_face_of_Britain.stm)

Beck, U. and Beck-Gernsheim, E. (2001) *Individualisation: institutionalised individualism and its social and political consequences*. London: Sage

Benhabib, S. and Cornell, D. (1987) *Feminism as Critique: essays on the politics of gender in late-capitalist societies*. Cambridge: Polity

Best, S. and Kellner, D. (1997) *The Postmodern Turn*. New York: Guildford Press

Bhabha, H. (1990) The third space. In J. Rutherford (ed) *Identity, Community, Culture, Difference*. London: Lawrence and Wishart

Bloomer, M. (1997) *Curriculum Making in Post-16 Education: the social conditions of studentship*. London: Routledge

Blumer, H. (1986) *Symbolic Interactionism: perspective and method.* Berkeley: University of California Press

Bordo, S. (1989) The body and the reproduction of femininity: a feminist appropriation of Foucault. In A. Jaggar and S. Bordo (eds) *Gender/Body/Knowledge: feminist reconstructions of being and knowing.* New Brunswick: Rutgers University Press

Bourdieu, P. (1977) *Outline of a Theory of Practice.* Cambridge: Cambridge University Press

Bourdieu, P. (1984) *Distinction: a social critique of the judgement of taste.* London: Routledge and Kegan Paul

Bourdieu, P. and Passeron, J. (1977) *Reproduction in Education, Society and Culture.* London: Sage

Brah, A. (1994) in H. Mirza (ed) *Black British Feminism: a reader.* London: Routledge.

Brah, A. (1996) *Cartographies of Diaspora: contesting identities.* London: Routledge

Brown, P. and Lauder, H. (2000) Education, child poverty and the politics of collective intelligence. In S. J. Ball (ed) *Sociology of Education: major themes,* Vol. IV: 1753-1779. London: Routledge

Brown, N., Corney, M. and Stanton, G. (2004) *Breaking out of the Silos: 14-30 education and skills policy.* London: Nigel Brown Associates

Burchell, G. (1993) Liberal government and techniques of the self. *Economy and Society.* 22(3): 267-282

Burman, I. and Parker, E. (1993) *Discourse Analytic Research: repertoires and readings of texts in action.* London: Routledge

Burr, V. (1995) *An Introduction to Social Constructionism.* London: Routledge

Butler, J. (1990/1999) *Gender Trouble: feminism and the subversion of identity.* New York: Routledge

Butler, J. (1993) *Bodies that Matter: on the discursive limits of 'sex'.* New York: Routledge

Caballero, C. (2007) 'Mixed' families: assumptions and new approaches. In J. M. Sims (ed) *Mixed Heritage: identity, policy and practice.* London: Runnymede

Camper, C. (2004) Into the mix. In J. O. Ifekwunigwe (ed) *'Mixed Race' Studies: a reader.* London: Routledge

Carby, H. (1982) White women listen! Black feminism and the boundaries of sisterhood. In The Centre for Contemporary Cultural Studies (eds) *The Empire Strikes Back: race and racism in 70s Britain.* London: Hutchinson

Childers and hooks, B. (1990) A conversation about race and class. In M. Hirsch and E. Fox Keller (eds) *Conflicts in Feminism.* New York: Routledge

Chiong, J. (1998) *Racial Categorization of Multiracial Children in Schools.* Westport, Connecticut: Bergen and Garvey

Clark, K. B. and Clark, M. K. (1939) The development of consciousness of self and the emergence of racial identity in Negro pre-school children. *Journal of Social Psychology,* 10: 591-599

Clark, K. B. and Clark, M. K. (1947) Racial identification and preference in Negro children. In T. Newcomb and E. Hartley (eds) *Readings in Social Psychology.* New York: Holt, Rinehart and Winston.

Coffield, F. (1999) Breaking the consensus: lifelong learning as social control. *British Education Research Journal,* 25(4): 479-499

Cole, M. and Hill, D. (1995) Games of despair and rhetorics of resistance: post-modernism, education and reaction. *British Journal of Sociology of Education,* 16(2): 165-182

Colley, H. and Hodkinson, P. (2001) Problems with *Bridging the Gap*: the reversal of structure and agency in addressing social exclusion. *Critical Social Policy,* 21(3): 335-359

Colley, H., James, D., Tedder, M., and Diment, K. (2003) Learning as becoming in vocational education and training: class, gender and the role of vocational habitus. *Journal of Vocational Education and Training,* 55 (4), 471-498

Connolly, P. (1998) *Racism, Gender Identities and Young Children: social relations in a multi-ethnic inner-city primary school.* London: Routledge

Daniel, R.G. (1996) Black and white identity in the new millennium: unsevering the ties that bind. In M. Root (ed) *The Multiracial Experience: racial borders as the new frontier.* Thousand Oaks, California: Sage

David, M. (2003) *Personal and Political.* Stoke-on-Trent: Trentham Books

Davies, B. (1990) *Frogs and Snails and Feminist Tales.* London: Allen and Unwin

Derrida, J. (1976) *Of Grammatology.* Baltimore: John Hopkins University Press

DES (1981) *West Indian Children in Our Schools.* Rampton Report London: HMSO

DES (1985) *Education for All: the report of the committee of inquiry into the education of children from ethnic minority groups.* Swann Report London: HMSO

DES (2003) *Challenging Racism: further education leading the way.* London: The Commission for Black Staff in Further Education

DfEE (1998) *The Learning Age: a renaissance for a new Britain.* London: The Stationery Office, Cmnd 3790

DfEE (1999) *Learning to Succeed: a new framework for post-16 learning.* London: The Stationery Office, Cmnd 4392

DfES (2002) *Success for All – Reforming Further Education and Training: our vision for the future.* London: HMSO

DfES (2003) *Aiming High: raising the achievement of minority ethnic pupils.* London

DfES (2004) *Understanding the Educational Needs of Mixed Heritage Pupils.* London: Research Report 549

DfES (2006) *Further Education: raising skills, improving life chances.* Norwich: HMSO

Erikson, E.H. (1968) *Identity, Youth and Crisis.* New York: Norton

European Commission (2001) *Making a European Area of Lifelong Learning a Reality.* Com 2001 (678)

Fatimilehin, I. A. (1999) Of jewel heritage: racial socialisation and racial identity attitudes amongst adolescents of mixed African-Caribbean/white parentage. *Journal of Adolescence*, 22: 303-318

Fergusson, R., Pye D., McLaughlin, E. and Muncie, J. (2000) Normalised dislocation and new subjectivities in post-16 markets for education and work. *Critical Social Policy*, 20(3): 283-305

Feuchtwang, S. (1990) Racism, territoriality and ethnocentricity. In A.X. Cambridge and S. Feuchtwang (eds) *Antiracist Strategies*. London: Avebury

Flax, J. (1990) Postmodernism and gender relations in feminist theory. In L. Nicholson (ed) *Feminism/Postmodernism*. New York: Routledge

Fordham, S. (1988) Racelessness as a factor in black students' school success: pragmatic strategy or pyrrhic victory. In S. J. Ball (ed) *Sociology of Education: major themes*, Vol. II: 660-697. London: Routledge

Foskett, N. and Hemsley Brown, J. (2001) *Choosing Futures: young people's decision-making in education, training and career markets*. London: Routledge Falmer

Foskett, N., Lumby, J. and Maringe, F. (2003) Pathways and progression at 16+: 'fashion', peer influence and college choice. Paper presented at the British Education Research Association Annual Conference, September 2003

Foucault, M. (1972) *The Archaeology of Knowledge*. London: Tavistock

Foucault, M. (1979) *Discipline and Punish: the birth of the prison*. Harmondsworth: Penguin

Francis, B. (1999a) You can never get too much education: the discourses used by secondary school students in their discussion of post compulsory education. *Research in Post-Compulsory Education*, 4(3): 305-319

Francis, B. (1999b) Modernist reductionism or post-structuralist relativism: can we move on? An evaluation of the arguments in relation to feminist educational research. *Gender and Education*, 11(4): 381-393

Francis, B. (2000) *Boys, Girls and Achievement*. London: Routledge

Frankenberg, R. (1993) *White Women, Race Matters: the social construction of whiteness*. Minneapolis: University of Minnesota Press

Frosh, S., Phoenix, A. and Pattman, R. (2002) *Young Masculinities: understanding boys in contemporary society*. Basingstoke: Palgrave

Fryer, R. (1997) *Learning for the 21st Century. First Report of the National Advisory Group for Continuing Education and Lifelong Learning*. London: NAGfELL

Furlong, A. and Cartmel, F. (1997) *Young People and Social Change: individualisation and risk in late modernity*. Milton Keynes: Open University Press

Gadamer, H. (1975) *Truth and Method*. London: Sheed and Ward

Gibbs, J. T. (1997) Biracial adolescents. In J. T. Gibbs and H. Larke-Nahme (eds) *Children of Color: psychological interventions with culturally diverse youth*. New York: Jossey-Bass

Gibbs, J. T. and Hines, A. (1992) Negotiating ethnic identity: issues for black-white biracial adolescents. In M. Root (ed) *Racially Mixed People in America*. Newbury Park, California: Sage

Gilbert, D. (2005) Interrogating mixed-race: a crisis of ambiguity? *Social Identities*, 11 (1): 55-74

Gillborn, D. (1995) *Racism and Anti-racism in Real Schools*. Buckingham: Open University Press

Gillborn, D. (1996) Student roles and perspectives in antiracist education: a crisis of white ethnicity? *British Educational Research Journal*, 22(2): 165-179

Gillborn, D. and Mirza, H. (2000) *Educational Inequality: mapping race, class and gender – a synthesis of research*. London: Ofsted

Gilroy, P. (1993) *Small Acts: thoughts on the politics of black culture*. London: Serpent's Tail

Gilroy, P. (2000) *Against Race: imagining political culture beyond the colour line*. Cambridge, Mass.: Belknap Press of Harvard University Press

Giroux, H. (1988) *Teachers as Intellectuals: towards a critical pedagogy of learning*. South Hadley, Mass.: Bergin and Garvey

Gist, N. and Dworkin, A. (1972) (eds) *The Blending of Races: marginality and identity in world perspective*. New York: Wiley-Interscience

Goldberg, D. T. (1993) *Racist Culture: philosophy and the politics of meaning*. Oxford: Blackwell

Goldthorpe, J. (1997) Problems of meritocracy. In H. Halsey, H. Lauder, P. Brown and A. Wells (eds) *Education: culture, economy, society*. Oxford: Oxford University Press

Gordon, C. (1991) Government rationality: an introduction. In G. Burchell, C. Gordon and P. Miller (eds) *The Foucault Effect: studies in governmentality*. London: Harvester Sheaf

Gordon, L.R. (1995) Critical 'mixed race?' in *Social Identities*, 1(2): 381-395

Greener, I. (2002) Agency, social theory and social policy. *Critical Social Policy*, 22(4): 688-705

The Guardian (1997) Beige Britain, 22 May, G2 section, p2

The Guardian (2003) Mixing It, 22 Feb, Guardian Weekend, p35

The Guardian (2006) Absent voices, 6 Sept, Society Guardian

Hall, S. (1992) The new ethnicities. In J. Donald and A. Rattansi (eds) *'Race', Culture and Difference*. London: Sage

Hammersley, M. (1993) *Educational Research: current issues*. London: Paul Chapman

Haraway, D. (1990) A manifesto for cyborgs: science, technology and socialist feminism in the 1980s. In L. Nicholson (ed) *Feminism/Postmodernism*. New York: Routledge

Hartsock, N. (1990) Foucault on power: a theory for women? In L. Nicholson (ed) *Feminism/Postmodernism*. New York: Routledge

Hodkinson, P., Sparks, A. C., and Hodkinson, H. (2000 [1996]) Career decision making and culture in the transition from school to work. In S. J. Ball (ed) *Sociology of Education: major themes*, Vol. I: 343-361. London: Routledge

Hornsby-Smith, M. (1993) Gaining access. In N. Gilbert (ed) *Researching Social Life*. London: Sage

Hutton, W. (1995) *The State We're In*. London: Jonathan Cape

Hyland, T. and Merrill, B. (2003) *The Changing Face of Further Education: lifelong learning, inclusion and community values in further education*. London: Routledge Falmer

Ifekwunigwe, J.O. (1997) Diaspora's daughters, Africa's orphans? In H. Mirza (ed) *Black British Feminism: a reader*. London: Routledge

Ifekwunigwe, J. O. (1999) *Scattered Belongings: cultural paradoxes of 'race', nation and gender*. London: Routledge

Ifekwunigwe, J. O. (2001) Re-membering 'race': on gender, 'mixed race' and family in the English-African diaspora. In D. Parker and M. Song (eds) *Rethinking 'Mixed Race'*. London: Pluto Press

Ifekwunigwe, J. O. (ed) (2004) *'Mixed Race' Studies: a reader*. London: Routledge

Jones, A. (1997) Teaching post-structuralist feminist theory in education: student resistances. *Gender and Education*, 9: 261-269

Jones, L. (2004) 'Is biracial enough (or what's this about a multiracial category on the census?: a conversation). In J. O. Ifekwunigwe (ed) *'Mixed Race' Studies: a reader*. London: Routledge

Katz, I. (1996) *The Construction of Racial Identity in Children of Mixed Parentage: mixed metaphors*. London: Jessica Kingsley

Keep. E. and Mayhew, K. (1998) Vocational education and training and economic performance. In T. Buxton, P. Chapman and P. Temple (eds) *Britain's Economic Performance*. London: Routledge

Keep, E. and Mayhew, K. (2000) Towards the knowledge-driven economy. *Renewal*, 7(4): 50-59

Kennedy, H. (1997) *Learning Works: widening participation in further education*. Coventry: FEFC

Killeen, J., Turton, R., Diamond, W., Dosnon, O. and Wach, M. (1999) Education and the labour market: subjective aspects of human capital investment. *Journal of Education Policy*, 14(2): 99-116

Klatch, R.E. (1987) *Women of the New Right*. Philadelphia: Temple University Press

Laclau, E. and Mouffe, C. (1985) *Hegemony and Socialist Strategy: towards a radical democratic politics*. London: Verso

Leathwood, C. (1998) Technological futures: gendered visions of learning? *Research in Post-Compulsory Education*, 4(1), 5-22

Lewis, R. (2004) Seminar paper: Mixed: what the census can tell us, Institute of Education, University of London, June 2004

Lincoln, Y. S. and Guba, E. G. (1985) *Naturalistic Enquiry*. Beverly Hills, California: Sage

Lister, R. (2001) New Labour: a study in ambiguity from a position of ambivalence. *Critical Social Policy*, 21(4): 425-447

Lovibond, S. (1983) Feminism and postmodernism. *New Left Review*, no.178

Lucey, H. and Walkerdine, V. (1999) Boys' underachievement, social class and changing masculinities. In T. Cox (ed) *Combating Educational Disadvantage*. London: Falmer Press

Mac an Ghaill, M. (1999) *Contemporary Racisms and Ethnicities: social and cultural transformations*. Philadelphia, Penn.: Open University Press

MacPherson, C. B. (1962) *The Political Theory of Possessive Individualism: Hobbes to Locke*. Oxford: Clarendon Press

Maguire, M., Macrae, M. and Ball, S. J. (1999) Promotion, persuasion and class-taste: marketing (in) the UK post-compulsory sector. *British Journal of Sociology of Education*, 20(3): 291-308

Mahtani, M. (2002) What's in a name? *Ethnicities,* 2(4): 469-490

Mahtani, M. and Moreno, A. (2001) Same difference: towards a more unified discourse in 'mixed race' theory. In D. Parker and M. Song (eds) *Rethinking 'Mixed Race'*. London: Pluto Press

McNay, L. (1992) *Foucault and Feminism*. Cambridge: Polity

McRobbie, A. (2000) *Feminism and Youth Culture* (2nd Edition). London: MacMillan Press

Miles, R. (1989) *Racism*. London: Routledge

Mirza, H. (1992) Young, Female and Black. London: Routledge

Mirza, H. (ed) (1997) *Black British Feminism: a reader*. London: Routledge

Mizen, P. (2003) The best days of your life: youth, policy and Blair's New Labour. *Critical Social Policy,* 23(4), 453-476

Modood, T., Berthoud, R., Lakey, J., Nazroo, J., Smith, P., Virdee, S. and Beishon, S. (1997) *Ethnic Minorities in Britain: diversity and disadvantage. The Fourth National Survey of Ethnic Minorities*. London: Policy Studies Institute

Mohanty, C. (2003) *Feminism Without Borders: decolonizing theory, practicing solidarity.* Durham: Duke University Press

Mouffe, C. (1995) Feminism, citizenship, and radical democratic politics. In L. Nicholson and N. Seidman (eds) *Social Postmodernism: beyond identity politics*. Cambridge, Mass.: Cambridge University Press

Murphy, J. (1993) A degree of waste: the economic benefits of educational expansion. *Oxford Review of Education*, 19(1): 9-31

Nagel, J. (1996) *American Indian Ethnic renewal: red power and the resurgence of identity and culture*. New York: Oxford University Press

Nicholson, L. and Seidman, N. (eds) (1995) *Social Postmodernism: beyond identity politics.* Cambridge Mass, Cambridge University Press

Nightingale, D.J. and Cromby, J. (eds) (1999) *Social Constructionist Psychology: a critical analysis of theory and practice.* Buckingham: Open University Press

Olesen, V. (1998) Feminisms and models of qualitative research. In N. K. Denzin and Y. S. Lincoln (eds) *Landscape of Qualitative Research.* London: Routledge

Olumide, J. (2002) *Raiding the Gene Pool: the social construction of mixed race.* Sterling, Virginia: Pluto Press

Olumide, G. (2005) Mixed race children. In T. Okitikpi (ed) *Working with Children of Mixed Parentage.* Lyme Regis, Dorset: Russell House Publishing

Olumide, J. (2007) People in Harmony. In J. M. Sims (ed) *Mixed Heritage: identity, policy and practice.* London: Runnymede

Omi, M. and Winant, H. (1994) *Racial formation in the United States: from the 1960s to the 1990s.* New York: Routledge

Owen, C. (2001) 'Mixed race' in official statistics. In D. Parker and M. Song (eds) *Rethinking 'Mixed Race'.* London: Pluto Press

Owen, C. (2004) Seminar paper: Mixed: what the census can tell us, Institute of Education, University of London, June 2004

Ozga, J. (1990) Policy research and policy theory: a comment on Fitz and Halpin. *Journal of Education Policy,* 5(4): 359-62

Ozga, J. (2000) *Policy Research in Educational Settings.* Buckingham: Open University Press

Parekh, B. (2000) *The Commission on the Future of Multi-Ethnic Britain: report of the commission on the future of multi-ethnic Britain.* Runnymede Trust. London: Profile

Park, R. (1952) *Human Communities.* New York: Free Press

Park, R. (1964) *Race and Culture.* New York: Free Press

Parker, D. and Song, M. (1995) Commonality and difference and the dynamics of disclosure in depth interviewing. *Sociology,* 29(2): 241-256

Parker, D. and Song, M. (2001) Introduction: rethinking 'mixed race'. In D. Parker and M. Song, M. (eds) *Rethinking 'Mixed Race'.* London: Pluto Press

Parker, I. (1992) *Discourse Dynamics: critical analysis for social and individual psychology.* London: Routledge

Parker, I. and the Bolton Discourse Network (1999) *Critical Textwork: an introduction to varieties of discourse and analysis.* New York: Open University Press

Peters, M. (1996) *Poststructuralism, Politics and Education.* Connecticut: Bergin and Garvey

Phoenix, A. (1997) 'I'm white! So what?' The construction of whiteness for young Londoners. In M. Fine, L. Weiss, L. Powell and L. Mun Wong (eds) *Off White: readings on race, power and society.* London: Routledge.

Rabinow, P. (ed) (1986) *The Foucault Reader.* Harmondsworth: Penguin

Raggatt, P. and Williams, S. (1999) *Government, Markets and Vocational Qualifications: an anatomy of policy.* London: Falmer Press

Rattansi, A. (1992) Changing the subject? Racism, culture and education. In J. Donald and A. Rattansi (eds) *'Race', Culture and Difference.* London: Sage

Rattansi, A. (1995) Just framing: ethnicities and racisms in a 'postmodern' framework. In L. Nicholson and N. Seidman (eds) *Social Postmodernism: beyond identity politics.* Cambridge, Mass: Cambridge University Press

Razack, S. (1998) *Looking White People in the Eye: gender, race, and culture in courtrooms and classrooms.* Toronto: University of Toronto Press

Reay, D. (1998) *Class Work: mothers' involvement in their children's primary schooling.* London: UCL Press

Reay, D. (2000 [1998]) Rethinking social class: qualitative perspectives on class and gender. In S. J. Ball (ed) *Sociology of Education: major themes,* Vol. II: 990-1008. London: Routledge

Reay, D. and Ball, S. J. (1997) 'Spoilt for choice': the working classes and education markets. *Oxford Review of Education,* 23: 89-101

Reay, D., Davies, J., David, M. and Ball, S. J. (2001) Choice of degree or degrees of choice? Class, 'race' and the higher education choice process. *Sociology,* 35(4): 855-874

Reiss, H. (ed) (1991) *Kant: Political Writings.* Cambridge: Cambridge University Press

Rockquemore, K. A. and Brunsma, D. (2002) *Beyond Black: biracial identity in America.* Thousand Oaks, California: Sage

Root, M. (ed) (1992) *Racially Mixed People in America.* Newbury Park, California: Sage

Root, M. (1996) The multiracial experience: racial borders as a significant frontier in race relations. In M. Root (ed) *The Multiracial Experience: racial borders as the new frontier.* Thousand Oaks, California: Sage

Rose, N. (1992) Governing the enterprising self. In P. Heelas and P. Morris (eds) *The Values of the Enterprise Culture: the moral debate.* London: Routledge

Sanchez, G. G. (2004) Y Tu Que? (Y2K): Latino history in the new millennium. In J. O. Ifekwunigwe (ed) *'Mixed Race' Studies: a reader.* London: Routledge

Schwandt, T. A. (1998) Constructivist, interpretivist approaches to human inquiry. In N. K. Denzin and Y. S. Lincoln (eds) *Landscape of Qualitative Research.* London: Sage

Scott, J. (1990) *A Matter of Record: documentary sources in social research.* Cambridge: Polity

SEU (Social Exclusion Unit) (1999) *Bridging the Gap: new opportunities for 16-18 year-olds not in education, employment or training.* London: The Stationery Office, Cm 4405

Shackleton, J. (1992) *Training too much? A sceptical look at the economics of skills provision in the UK.* London: Institute of Economic Affairs

Silverman, D. (1993) *Interpreting Qualitative Data: methods for analysing talk, text and interaction.* London: Sage

Skeggs, B. (1994) Situating the production of feminist methodology. In M. Maynard and J. Purvis (eds) *Researching Women's Lives for a Feminist Perspective.* London: Taylor and Francis

Skeggs, B. (1997) *Formations of Class and Gender: becoming respectable.* London: Sage

Skinner, D. (2004) Racialised futures: biologism and the changing politics of identity. Paper presented at British Sociological Association Annual Conference, March 2004

Small, S. (1994) *Racialised Barriers: the black experience in the United States and England in the 1980s.* London; New York: Routledge

Soper, K. (1993) Postmodernism, subjectivity and the question of value. In J. Squires (ed) *Principled Positions: postmodernism and the rediscovery of value.* London: Routledge

Stacey, J. (1988) Can there be a feminist ethnography? *Women's Studies International Forum,* 11(1): 21-27

Stonequist, E. V. (1937) *The Marginal Man: a study of personality and culture conflict.* New York: Russell and Russell

Tessman, L. (1999) The racial politics of mixed race. *Journal of Social Philosophy,* 30(2): 276-294

Tight, M. (1998a) Education, education, education! The vision of lifelong learning in the Kennedy, Dearing and Fryer Reports. *Oxford Review of Education,* 24(4): 473-485

Tight, M. (1998b) Lifelong Learning: opportunity or compulsion? *British Journal of Educational Studies,* 46(3), 251-63

Tizard, B. and Phoenix, A. (2001[1993]) *Black, White or Mixed race: race and racism in the lives of young people of mixed parentage.* London: Routledge

Tomlinson, S. (2001) *Education in a Post-Welfare Society.* Buckingham: Open University Press

Usher, R. (1996) A critique of the neglected epistemological assumptions of educational research. In D. Scott and R. Usher (eds) *Understanding Educational Research.* London: Routledge

Volman, M. and Ten Dam, G. (1998) Equal but different: contradictions in the development of gender identity in the 1990s. *British Journal of Sociology of Education,* 19(4), 529-545

Walkerdine, V. (1990) *Schoolgirl Fictions.* London: Verso

Ware, V. (1991) *Beyond the Pale: white women, racism, and history.* London: Verso

Warmington, P. (2002) Taking out insurance against 'the learning age': the simultaneity of consent, antagonism and transcendence in mature students' participation in access to HE. Paper presented at Discourse Power Resistance Conference, April 2002

Weekes, D. (1997) Shades of blackness: young black female constructions of beauty. In H. Mirza (ed) *Black British Feminism: a reader.* London: Routledge

Whelelan, I. (1995) *Modern Feminist Thought: from the second wave to post-feminism.* Edinburgh: Edinburgh University Press

Whitty, G., Power, S. and Halpin, D. (1997) *Devolution and choice in education: the school, the state, and the market.* Buckingham: Open University Press

Williams, T. (1996) Race as process: reassessing the 'what are you?' encounters of biracial individuals. In M. Root (ed) *The Multiracial Experience: racial borders as the new frontier.* Thousand Oaks, California: Sage

Wilson, A. (1987) *Mixed Race Children: a study of identity.* London: Allen and Unwin

Winters, L. and DeBose H. (2003) *New Faces in a Changing America: multiracial identity in the 21st century.* Thousand Oaks, California: Sage

Women and Equality Unit (2004) *Minority and Ethnic Women in the UK.* London: DTI

Zack, N. (1995) *American Mixed Race: the culture of microdiversity.* London: Rowman and Littlefield

Zera, A. and Jupp, T. (2000) Widening participation. In A. Smithers and P. Robinson (eds) *Further Education Re-formed.* London: Falmer

Index